Stop Surviving!
&
Start Thriving!

The Biblical Science of Riches

By Ashley Meece

Plus, 101 ways to save money!

- Do we have to live life as paupers to be godly?
- Is it wrong to have money?
- Is it sinful to be rich?
- Do you need a lot of money to make money?

Simply,

No!

The Command

"Be kindly affectioned one to another with brotherly love; in honour preferring one another. **Not slothful in business;** fervent in spirit; serving the Lord." Romans 12:10, 11 *(Note: my underline)*

This is a command that is often overlooked. You may not have a desire to do this. It is still a command!

Premise

-When does it become wrong to have money?

The sin comes when you become greedy or covetous. We are to serve Christ, not our own selfish interests. Putting Christ first – especially in our finances, is not an option, but a command (Matthew 6:33). You are only as spiritual as you are financially honest.

This book is written to be helpful so that you can serve Christ better. If you are not sure that if you were to die today you would go to heaven, skip to the appendix and find that out for sure. The riches on this earth are nothing compared to the riches of heaven.

Disclaimer

ISBN-13: 978-1500746148

ISBN-10: 1500746148

Ashley Meece Publication

Copyright 2014

All selections are from the King James Version

Editors: Sandra Furr, Steven Hutchinson, David Meece

Contents

Chapter

1

Minding the Herd

Or

Where did it all go?

Money Story- When I was young, we owned goats. One night, through an unfortunate turn of events, one goat escaped. We chased it through the field with a truck trying to catch it. No such luck. Eventually, we recovered it when we put an ad in the paper. Apparently, it got hungry and decided to eat our neighbor's roses. We sold the goat to the neighbor because they had made it their pet and wanted to keep it.

Lesson Learned- Make sure your money and property do not "escape" when you're not looking. Keep a watchful eye on your assets.

What does the Bible say about money?

Money Verses- "Be thou diligent to know the state of thy flocks, and look well to thy herds." Proverbs 27:23

- "The rich man had exceeding many flocks and herds:" 2 Samuel 12:2

- The people in Bible days raised animals for food, as well as, for money. This was their livelihood. A man with many animals was very rich. (See Job, Abraham, etc.)

How do I use what the Bible teaches?

1. Know how much money you have or do not have.

- Find out where your money is, how much you have, and where it goes. Add it up. Give your things real market value. Do not base this on your purchase price. Almost everything loses value when it is no longer new.

2. You should know your true assets (herds and flocks) and true liabilities.

- People who are experiencing financial troubles usually have no idea where their money goes.

How can you know the difference between an asset and a liability?

- This is easy. That which produces income is an asset. That which produces expense is a liability.

- An true asset is something that brings money in (income) without work on your part (except cashing the check).

- A liability is anything else or that which generates expense.

- Liabilities are things that take up space in the garage, attic, or basement. They are things that you bought that are not generating income or that may be costing you money. It could be that the liabilities are the garage, basement, and attic. I am saying it could be your house.

3. Ask yourself, after you have completely assessed the situation, "Is this where I want to be? Do I have a real plan to prosper God's way? Am I happy with where I am?" There is nothing wrong with being happy where you are. Those of you who are struggling to pay the bills need to get busy – not with another job or self-employment, but truly working for yourself.

- There are many verses in the Bible about money. These are just a few verses that teach the importance of money.

Money Verses -"Charge them that are rich in this world, that they be not highminded, nor trust in uncertain riches, but in the living God, who giveth us richly all things to enjoy." 1 Tim 6:17

- Do not trust in uncertain riches, but trust in the living God. He, as our loving heavenly Father, wants us to prosper in true riches. When Joseph was financially broke, he was called a prosperous man. (Genesis 39:2, 3, & 23) God's prosperity isn't about being "filthy rich". It's about God blessing all that you do because you trust in Him.

A Christian should not trust in money. It is far better to trust in God who has everything and can give you what you need. Remember God is the source of all that we have. Put Him first!

God should be first in every area of your life. He is not to be your co-pilot He is to be your pilot. He should have first say and last say in your life. Never should money, things, family, friends, or self be first. He is our all. We have nothing good that He has not given us.

Money Verses-"So likewise, whosoever he be of you that forsaketh not all that he hath, he cannot be my disciple." Luke 14:33

Do not hold the things of this world dear. Christ should always come first.

"If therefore ye have not been faithful in the unrighteous mammon, who will commit to your trust the true riches?" Luke 16:11

- Who shall commit to your trust the true riches if you are mishandling the money God has given you?

- "And the lord commended the unjust steward, because he had done wisely: for the children of this world are in their generation wiser than the children of light." Luke 16:8

- The children of this world are wiser than the children of light! Isn't it a bad testimony when lost people of this world have a better financial score than believers?

- Too many Christians are sadly – broke. I think it's time that we learned what the Bible says about handling money.

Money Verse

Read it in the Bible for yourself in Matthew 25:14-30

- In the story of the talents and the servants, we see that our Lord expects a return on investment. One of the servants is reprimanded when he does not invest the talent he was given. God did not bless the laziness, fear, or flattery of that servant.

- At the same time, it is not greediness to invest. We know this because the servant in the parable represents us. Christ is represented by the Lord of the servants. Christ is not greedy to ask for a return on his investment from us. He wants us to **give** and **invest**. In return, we will have abundance (vs.29).

Materialism or Expensive Things - You should not need expensive things. If you have a spending problem, earning more money is not the answer. Conquer this problem before you start. I did not write this so that you can accumulate expensive things.

Money Verse - "Blessed are the poor in spirit: for theirs is the kingdom of heaven." Matthew 5:3

- I have heard many definitions of this verse. One way I think this verse can be applied is: we are happy if we have wealth, yet, we don't flaunt this wealth. This is being truly "poor in spirit" and not showing off.

Keeping Up With the Joneses- This is a trap many people fall into. They try to flaunt wealth that they do not have. In the attitude or spirit of "Look at me! I'm rich!" We should have the attitude or spirit of a humble, poor person no matter how rich we are! Many people have this definition completely backwards. They do not have money, but they try to keep up appearances by going into further debt.

Mindfulness –This is scheduled time to think. It is not meditation. You should take at the least fifteen minutes a day to think. Notice I did not say worry. You need actual time set aside to think about your problems and your life. Take notes. You may not solve your problems the first time. Write down any progress you've made. If you think of a problem during the day, that you can put off, write it down. You may find that you worry less when using this method, simply because, you know you will have a scheduled time to think about it. You may plan on thinking about specific problems. That is great. Have a scheduled time each day for your problem until you solve it.

Budgeting Expenses - There are three areas that we need to pay special attention to when budgeting our money. These are listed in the order of importance. They are giving, saving, & investing.

Chapter

2

The Budget and Giving

Money Story - There was a poor blind beggar on the road one day. He heard a carriage pull up. It was the Rajah. The blind beggar was expecting a generous donation. He was surprised by this question. "What will you give to the Rajah?" The old, poor, beggar man was immediately angry. He thought to himself, "I have nothing beside this small bowl of rice. The Rajah has palaces filled with gold. Why should I give the Rajah anything?" So, he reached in his little bowl and pulled out one little grain of rice – his gift to the Rajah. The Rajah asked again, "What will you give to the Rajah?" The beggar man was disgusted. He, again, drew out a single grain of rice. The Rajah asked again, "What will you give to the Rajah?" The old beggar man was livid. He took another single grain of rice and gave it to the Rajah. The Rajah got back in his carriage and drove away. The old beggar man went back to eating his bowl of rice. He was almost through when at the bottom he found three nuggets of gold – a gift from the Rajah.

Lesson Learned- Sometimes, we are too greedy to see a real opportunity. We will never know how many opportunities we have missed because we were blinded by greed.

Giving- 10%

Money Verse -"Will a man rob God? Yet ye have robbed me. But ye say, Wherein have we robbed thee? In tithes and offerings. Ye are cursed with a curse: for ye have robbed me, even this whole nation. Bring ye all the tithes into the store house, that there may be meat in my house, and prove me now herewith, sayeth the LORD of hosts, if I will not open you the windows of heaven, and pour you out a blessing, that there shall not be room enough to receive it." Malachi 3:8-10

- The first ten percent of your income is to give away. This is the most important part of your finances, but, to whom shall we give it?

- God tells us in his word to give the tenth part to him. Do not rob God. Malachi 3:8-10. Giving keeps your view of you and others in perspective. Tithing keeps greed at bay!

- You **need** to give more than this 10%, but, make sure it comes out of your "mad money", that is, what you have left after paying the bills. This is called an offering. You should always give an offering when you give your tithe. How much is up to the individual.

- Even a non-church goer, should give the first ten percent to a charity. Tithing and charitable giving are one way the economy circulates money. The economy depends on charity as part of the circulation of money. The more money that circulates, the stronger the economy.

- For example, you get paid, and then you give. The money circulates, then, comes back to you with friends both monetarily and physically. (Luke 16:9).You sow to the wind, you reap the whirl wind (Hosea 8:7). This is Biblical, and also the way capitalism works. You sow then you reap. YOU SOW THEN REAP IS GOD'S UNIVERSAL LAW!!! (Galatians 6:7).This is the money cycle. It is one thing of importance in circulating money in the economy.

- For example, you are a garbage collector. You give your church $100.00 in the offering plate. This helps pay the pastor and the assistant pastor and missionaries around the world, also, the electric company, the water company, and the sewage company. It pays all the people who work for those companies. They all buy groceries, cars, houses, and clothes. It pays the grocery store employees, the trucks that deliver the groceries, the gas for the trucks, the people that grow the groceries. Then, it pays for the car, the salesman's commission, the truck drivers that deliver the car, the manufacturing plant, the iron and steel worker, the paint chemist, and the glass worker. Next, it supports the housing market and the clothing market. This could go on almost forever! (Have you noticed? They all have garbage that needs collecting?)

Chapter

3

The Budget and Saving

Money Story - The story of the grasshopper and the ant.

- The little ant worked all summer. The grasshopper played all summer. The grasshopper mocked the little ant. He thought the little ant was foolish for working and saving when he could be playing. The ant tried to tell him about the winter, but, the grasshopper had never seen a winter. He just laughed at the ant. When the winter came, the ant had food and shelter. The grasshopper did not. The grasshopper asked the little ant to share his food and shelter. The ant refused. He could not share his food because he only had enough for himself.

Lesson Learned- If we are not saving because we are lazy we will come to retirement (winter) penniless. Then, we will have to rely on the charity of others.

Money Verse - "Go to the ant thou sluggard; consider her ways, and be wise: Which having no guide, overseer, or ruler, Provideth her meat in the summer, and gathereth her food in the harvest." Proverbs 6:6-8

Savings – 10% - Put money in a safe place. You are getting older every single second. You need to save for retirement as well as for a rainy day. Saving is necessary in case your investments fail at the end of your life - Luke 16:9. You can save in many ways: The bank, bonds, silver, and gold. You will probably get a small return of a few percent. One way you should not save is having extra withheld from your tax withholding. Do not let the government save your money. They give you nothing for it.

Money Story - There was a little boy who got his hand stuck in a very expensive vase. They tried everything to get his hand out. They even called the fire department. No one could get the little boy's hand out of the priceless vase. Regrettably, after many hours, they decided they had to break the expensive vase. When they got the vase off, they found out why the boy's hand would not come out. His fist was clinched around a single penny.

Lesson Learned- You can be too cheap. Sometimes, people trying to save money will end up wasting money trying to save it. The old adage is "penny wise, pound foolish."

Chapter

4

The Budget and Investing

Money Story - The story goes that, one day, a young George Washington was walking in the garden. He noticed an unusual sight. The leaf lettuce had come up in the shape of his name "George Washington" He was so excited he called for his father. He said "Father, did you do that?" George's father said "George, why do you think anyone planted them like that? Is it because of the design?" "Yes, father." replied George. "You're right, George," said his father, "I did design it. I planted the seed in the shape of your name. I wanted to teach you that everything in this world has been designed – much more detailed than that lettuce patch. There must be a designer."

Lesson Learned- Lettuce is a good example of an asset. Lettuce can be the easiest vegetable to grow. It is the closest vegetable to an asset. You will never get lettuce, unless, you invest lettuce seed in the ground. You will get back more than you put in - if you have planted right. You will never get a return on any investment that you never invested. (No one will be legitimately contacting you from Nigeria needing you to send them money so you can get more money back. That is a scam.)

- The story is an example of something else. There is a designer of this world. God made the world. It is too intricately designed not to be created.

Investments- 10% - This is acquiring assets. (Ecclesiastes11:1-3). An asset is something that brings money in without work on your part (except cashing the check). A liability is anything else. Initial work may be required to set up the company, so that you do not have to continue to operate the business as the manager. If you have to constantly work to get your money, you have a part time/full time, self-employed job - which is a time liability. Here is one way to make an asset. Buy or start a business. It may have a small to large profitability. Next, hire a manager to do your job. He sends you the check every month. Now you have an asset.

- Another form of investing is to buy only parts of companies and allow the other partner (usually with the majority share of 51% or more) to run the company. He does all the work and you collect your share of the rewards.

- Loaning people or businesses money.

- You should not buy a business unless you can make it self-run with employees and a manager (automated works, too). A vending machine is the best example of a completely self-run company. Remember, it's not an asset until you don't have to work for it and you still get returns on your investment. Make sure you get a reasonable return on your investment. Investing is buying businesses that can be turned into assets.

Money Verse - "In the morning sow thy seed, and in the evening withhold not thine hand: for thou knowest not whether shall prosper, either this or that, or whether they both shall be alike good." Ecclesiastes11:6

Do Not Put All Your Eggs in One Basket- When you invest make sure you do not put all your money into one investment, in case that investment fails. Also, do not invest with just one person should that person you trusted turn out to be a crook. Do not invest in one type of investment because some markets do have down turns.

Chapter

5

The Win-Win Deal

Money Story- Recently, I was in need of a car. I was looking everywhere. On the way to town, my grandma and I spotted a beautiful Crown Victoria on the side of the road for sale. We investigated. The man selling it had repeatedly been offered much less than the car was worth. He was so disgusted he gave us a very fair price, just because we were willing to pay what he was asking. I have never owned a better car for reliability. It was a win-win deal. He sold his car for a decent price and I bought a great car.

Lesson Learned- If I had tried to swindle the owner of the car, I would have only hurt my own interests. If you go around trying to swindle and cheat people, no one will cry when you get swindled.

The Win-Win Deal- Every deal that you make will not be perfect. Do your best to be fair. Never cheat anyone. Try to make deals where no one loses. Happy people will remember that you did right by them. They will be happy to work with you again. You will feel better about yourself if you are honest. Never do a deal where you have to deceive someone in a negative way. I am not talking about a surprise birthday party. I am talking about a rotten deal. What I call a win-win deal is when both parties win and all participants are happy.

Do Not Rob the Poor- God gets very angry when anyone robs the poor. You do not have to be rich or poor to be a thief.

Money Verse -"Rob not the poor, because he is poor: neither oppress the afflicted in the gate: For the LORD will plead their cause, and spoil the soul of those that spoil them. " Proverbs 22:22, 23

Most Rich People Do Not Rob the Poor-There were two farmers that lived next to each other. The first was Farmer Full. He worked very hard on his field and planted many crops. His neighbor Farmer Fool was lazy. He did not plant crops. He never felt like it. One day, he was hungry, so, he decided to get a job with his neighbor Farmer Full. So his neighbor hired him. Farmer Fool hated his boss Farmer Full.

Farmer Full gave him orders while he made plans to hire more Farmer Fools and buy more fields. Farmer Fool was jealous. He was doing all the work and Farmer Full was getting all the wealth. He decided that he, Farmer Fool, deserved to be paid more. Farmer Fool demanded better wages. He felt the problem with his finances was his boss – that he, Farmer Fool, was being ripped off. His land was valuable. He could have planted. He just lacked initiative. He was not poor because of Farmer Full. He was poor because he was lazy. Did Farmer Full rob Farmer Fool? No, of course not. In the future Farmer Full may even decide to buy Farmer Fool's field.

Lesson Learned - Obviously, not everyone is a farmer. However, this can be applied to many types of businesses. The world is a bountiful place. The rich do not necessarily take from the poor. They simply harvest some of the bounty from the earth that the poor are too lazy to harvest. To be rich you do not necessarily have to make someone else poorer.

Money Verse -"I went by the field of the slothful, and by the vineyard of the man void of understanding; And, lo, it was all grown over with thorns, and nettles had covered the face thereof, and the stone wall thereof was broken down." Proverbs 24:31, 32

Hard Work- Don't misunderstand, I am for hard work, however; I am against going to work nearly every day and barely having enough to pay the bills. You need to use your hard work ethic and your brain.

Creating Wealth - A Lesson in Economics- You make a product (let's say it is a pair of shoes). Think of that product as a unit of wealth (how much it is worth). You sell it for a unit of wealth (cash), you trade that unit of wealth, plus, a few more units of wealth for another unit of wealth (lawn mower). When you made that first unit of wealth you became that much richer. There was that much more wealth in the world. Say for example, you imagine a product in your head. You design and make the product. You are paid in cash when you sell it at the store. You are a little bit richer. You buy someone else's product. You still are a little bit richer (especially if it's an asset). He buys someone else's product, and he is a little bit richer. Finally, the last person in the string buys your product again. You are all richer. Money is seen – not only with the eyes, but, truly with the mind.

Know Something about Economics.

You don't have to know as much as the secretary of the treasury, but you should know something.

Cash is King- Most of the time if you are having trouble closing a deal, pull out a wad of bills. Many times seeing the money will close the deal for you. Strangely enough, most people have a hard time saying no to cash money.

The Philosophy of Money

Money is just paper with ink on it. A million dollars is just a million pieces of paper. The thing that makes money worth something is that **you** think it is worth something! The sooner you realize this fact the less afraid of money and the less greedy you will be. When you stop thinking about money as valuable and start thinking about money as it truly is (paper) you can start to think clearly about making money through business.

Chapter

6

Investment Fraud

Money Story - Simple Simon decided that he would like to buy a business. He headed straight for Shady Sam. Shady Sam told Simple Simon about his wonderful business called "the Brooklyn Bridge." Shady Sam told Simple Simon about the wonderful toll money he receives every month. When Simple Simon invested, Shady Sam made like a banana and split taking with him all of Simple Simon's money.

Lesson Learned- Do not buy the Brooklyn Bridge. If it sounds too good to be true, it probably is. Most fraudulent people do not give you time to think it over. Do not buy something or go into a deal that has to be done "right now."

Money Story- When I was younger, we spotted an advertisement in the paper. A butcher was advertising whole cows for what we thought was cheap. You paid for the cow whole by the pound. However, we did not realize at the time how much waste there is. We truly paid much more than we should have. One of our friends suggested that we had paid double what we should have.

Lesson Learned- It is very, very, easy to get swindled. At the very least you could call the Better Business Bureau and find out if a company has a good rating before you buy into it. It may very well have problems that are hard to correct. Go into a deal with your eyes wide open.

Money Verses- "Envy not the oppressor, and choose none of his ways." Proverbs 3:31

"A false balance is an abomination to the LORD: but a just weight is his delight." Proverbs 11:1

- Do not fall for the "bait and switch." That is a confidence (con) man's favorite trick. He will lure you into one deal, and then, change to a bad deal at the last minute. He may also claim to have run out of the item. It can also be called "a shell game."

- Do not "buy a pig in a poke." Do not buy things sight unseen. If you do order it, it is best to pay for it after it is delivered. If you have a long standing relationship with someone, you may feel you can trust the person with whom you do business.

A Pyramid Scheme- Recently, a man tried this dastardly deed. It is very illegal. He took money from people and gave them a small amount back. They thought he had invested it and were giving them a return on this investment. He had not. Thinking that he had, they invited more friends to invest with them. He took their money (the second group) and gave part of it to the first group, etc. He spent most of the money on himself and his family members. He is now rightfully in jail.

Reinvesting Your Profits- When I make money with my investments, I put my new income back through the budget. I reinvest 10% of the money that I made and when that makes me money, I reinvest 10% of that money, etc. Relax, this is legal and safe.

Counterfeit- This is something that should go without saying. Buy things that are authentic. Make sure everything you buy is not stolen. This is what some would call "hot merchandise". If it is doubtful pass up the opportunity.

Do not "make money" (counterfeit bills). You will go to jail.

Do not rip anyone off and risk going to jail. There are too many good ways to make money legally.

Usury-The Bible instructs us not to charge usury of a fellow Christian. Usury is **excessive interest.** You are allowed to charge interest, just not excessive interest.

Money Verse- "In thee have they taken gifts to shed blood; thou hast taken usury and increase, and thou hast greedily gained of thy neighbours by extortion, and hast forgotten me, saith the Lord GOD." Ezekiel 22:12

Chapter

7

The Stock Market

Money Story- When I was younger, I dabbled in the markets. I was quickly disillusioned. I did have the right companies I found out later. They just weren't quite ready to take off yet. I did not lose too much. But I have not returned to the stock market since.

Lesson Learned- As a new inexperienced investor do not invest in the stock market unless you cannot possibly find anything else. It is like eating regurgitated food. So many people have bitten into it (or been bitten by it) and spit it out (rejected it) after it lost their money. This has happened so many times over, that many have come to accept it as normal. There is a bird that does that. It is called a vulture. She feeds her young regurgitated food. I respect the vulture, but I do not want to be one.

It Is Not Immoral- There is nothing sinful or immoral about the stock market. If you are experienced with the markets there is nothing wrong with investing in the markets. I simply warn those who are not market savvy, and do not know what they are doing.

The Stock Market Plays for Keeps- This is not a gamble. It is a risk on the assumption that the business you select will be successful during the time you invest.

Money Verse- "Boast not thyself of to morrow; for thou knowest not what a day may bring forth." Proverbs 27:1

Make a Mock Portfolio- If you decide that you do want to invest in the stock market practice a little first. Make a mock portfolio and track how you would have done if you had invested your real money in the market.

Yes, there are people who make money in the markets. I hope you are profitable, if you decide to invest. I decided long ago that for me there must be a better way.

Chapter

8

Time Liability

Money Story- We live on a dirt/gravel road. In the summertime, dust and dirt gets all over our cars. When we go into town, our car gets all filthy. If we go and wash it, the car gets dirty on the ride home. It is a waste of time and money.

Lesson Learned- A time liability is a waste of time and sometimes money.

Money Verse - "Labour not to be rich: cease from thine own wisdom." Proverbs 23:4

- This verse can be interpreted two ways.

1. Do not attempt to be rich. Do not try to gather wealth. God will make you rich. To try to get ahead is unwise.

Greed or the Love of Money

The Bible has much to say about greediness. It will eat you alive. Do not fall for one of Satan's best tricks. This is the root of all evil and it is deadly. (1 Timothy 6:10) Make sure you do not have a problem with this. Deal with this problem before you start. A person need not be rich to be greedy.

- The other way to interpret Proverbs 23:4 is a little more literal.

2. Working will not accomplish much more than paying the bills. You need to stop having the mindset that the only way to make money is to work at a job. That is unwise. You need to see that laboring at your job while scrimping and saving your money can be a time liability. A time liability is something that you don't want to do that eats up your time. For many people a time liability is their job or business. They will never have time to truly explore the possibilities. You will not be rich by manual labor. Cease from thine own wisdom. This is the downfall of many people. You need to learn to use your head.

Chapter

9

Can You Spot Yourself?

Money Story- When I was little I had a book where you could find hidden objects. I wouldn't always find everything, but I would usually find something.

Lesson Learned- You may not find yourself exactly in a scenario, but, you may find something that reminds you of you.

Scenario 1- In their haste to be rich or to care for their families they work many hours. They work like a slave. Maybe even at their business not at their job. You probably know this type of person. They are always busy. There is a line that they cross. I call it the "no point in being rich" line. They spend no time with their spouse or kids. They can buy a mocha whenever they want, but, they feel guilty after they drank it, because they gain weight. So, they go to the gym and work out. They buy their families lavish gifts. They live in the nicest house on the block and drive the nicest car. Yet, they never realize how much time they spend doing things they don't want to do. They hope that they will retire and get to enjoy it. The problem with that theory is they mistreat their body and when they get to retirement age they have such bad health they cannot enjoy it. The car rusts. The house may be foreclosed upon. Perhaps, even their identity may be stolen. Worse yet the money is all taken at the end of their life by the nursing homes. Time is much more valuable than money. Spend it wisely. Jesus says something about this person.

Money Verse - "Lay not up for yourselves treasures upon earth where moth and rust doth corrupt, and where thieves break through and steal: But lay up for yourselves treasures in heaven, where neither moth, nor rust doth corrupt, and where thieves do not break through nor steal:" Matthew 6:19, 20

Scenario 2 - This person is greedy. They just want more and more money. They have no plan for their money, other than to squander it. They will cheat, steal, lie, or anything else for money.

Money Verse -"The love of money is the root of all evil." 1 Timothy 6:10

Scenario 3 - This person owns one business or works one job. They pour all their time and money into one business or job. They get some satisfaction from their job or business. However, they are laboring to be rich. This person works for their money. As found in this verse, there is nothing wrong with this person's philosophy – to a point.

Money Verse - "For even when we were with you, this we commanded you, that if any would not work, neither should he eat." 2 Thessalonians 3:10

- However, I want to do more than just earn my food.

Scenario 4 - This person likes expensive things. They waste their money on stuff they do not truly need. The shame is that they spent their time working just to buy junk that they do not need. Some level of luxury is fun for a time, but try not to spoil yourself. Whatever you do, do not spoil your kids. You will regret that forever.

Money Verses -"But God said unto him, Thou fool, this night thy soul shall be required of thee: then whose shall those things be, which thou hast provided? So is he that layeth up treasure for himself, and is not rich toward God." Luke 12:20, 21(Note: my underline) Read the whole story for yourself in Luke 12:16-21

- "And he said unto them, Take heed; and beware of covetousness: for a man's life consisteth not in the abundance of the things which he posseth" Luke 12:15

Scenario 5 - This person has it together. They buy or develop new products and companies. They spend minimal time at their job which is simply setting up their system of running their companies. They understand the importance of time. They may occasionally make a mistake in running one of their companies, but they can correct it easily. They have time for their families and friends. They do not spend their time working in a big box (their work), then going home to a small box (house), in their even smaller box (car), only to have their body placed in an even smaller box (casket) when they die. You need to truly think outside the box (or boxes).

Chapter

10

The Rich Do Not Pay Taxes

Money Story- Simple Simon decided to go into politics. Simple Simon was angry at Rich Riley, "He is greedy," he said. "He does not pay his fair share of tax money. He never shares his money with the poor. I will share Rich Riley's money with the poor." So, Simple Simon raised the taxes on Rich Riley. He noticed that the price of Rich Riley's goods went up, but, Rich Riley was just as rich as before. Is Simple Simon frustrated? Not at all! He will do it again in a month or so. The poor will vote Simple Simon in again because the majority of voters are poor or middle class. After all prices are going up and we need more of Simple Simon's "free" money. Rich Riley just shakes his head in disbelief. He would gladly teach the poor to become rich. Yet, sadly, they despise Rich Riley. So, the story goes on for years, and years without anyone realizing how Simple Simon gets his money. He is a classic Robin Hood character. He "steals from the rich and gives to the poor". While in reality he is only robbing the poor, and then, giving them part of their money back. Of course, only after he pays for his yacht, his house, his car, and his divorce settlement. (Can you say pyramid scheme?)

Lesson Learned- The rich are not your enemy. More often than not, they are trying to give their customers a good deal. Many rich people give large portions of their wealth away; Of course, when they die they give it all away.

Money Verses- "The crown of the wise is their riches: but the foolishness of fools is folly." Proverb 14:24

" The rich man's wealth is his strong city: the destruction of the poor is their poverty." Proverbs 10:15

The Rich Do Not Pay Taxes - The poor and middle class pay almost all the taxes. Why do I say this? Business owners (the rich) pass the tax bill along to their customers (mostly the poor). I am not just talking about sales tax. Every business tax in existence is truly paid by the customer. No customers, no business. No business, no tax.

You Pay Way More Than You Think- Since we now know that the consumer pays everything, how much does he truly pay? I am not smart enough to figure that out. But, as nearly as I can tell you pay 50% or more in taxes when you add up all the taxes that are passed along to you the customer. Imagine a world without taxes. Everything would be half-price or less.

Chapter
11
The House of Cards
Or
The Budget, the Bills, and Debt

- When you were a kid, did you ever try to build a house out of cards? If you answered yes, you will know how hard it is to do so. The material is not sturdy. Similarly, many people try to build a house of cards (bad debt and liabilities) in their financial lives. The result is the same. Their financial house of debt, like a house of cards, falls most of the time. Why does it fall? They may think the debt they have is a reasonable amount. Then, sadly, they lose a job or an unexpected bill comes up. Then, they start living on their credit cards, sometimes, with no job. They watch in horror as their financial house of cards falls. The circumstances are always different, but the results are always the same. The fallout is not just financial. Even more sadly, many relationships are destroyed. Most divorce is over money. Money touches many other areas of our lives. See Matthew 7:24-27

Money Story - When I was younger they sent me many applications for credit cards. The interest was of course highway robbery. I have never needed a credit card. I can only remember once, when I had to borrow money from a relative. It was only a few hundred dollars.

Lesson Learned- The metal color of the plastic credit card you have does not define your financial standing or your financial life.

- Life is not about your credit score. You should not base your wealth on how much you are able to borrow. I do not even know what my credit score is. If you do know what your score is, I would guess that you have at some time in your life had debt. If this is how you judge your wealth, you need to redefine your success.

- Most kids think the credit card is a rite of passage into the teen years, along with a car. Do not do this to your child. Do not give them a credit card. They do not need a good credit score. They do need to learn strong character. They need character more than they need a car, a job, or their own apartment. Most of the failures in people's lives are directly related to their character flaws. Once you are an adult, they are hard to fix.

Money Story- Our friend Simple Simon is back again. Simple Simon needs to finance his car that he "has to have." So he puts it on a credit card. He tells his boss that he "has to have" a raise because living expenses have gone up. Next, Simple Simon buys a house. He has good credit so why not? He deserves the American dream. He goes to his boss again. Simple Simon is getting more and more in debt. He is building "a house of cards" or a "sand castle" without realizing it. Then one day Simple Simon is laid off. His wife leaves him because "he" lost the house, the car, and all of their other "assets".

Lesson Learned- I have seen "the house of cards" so many times it makes me ill. The circumstances aren't always the same, but "the house of cards" is. Strangely enough, the people who have lost it all still do not go into business because it is too risky.

Bills- Some budgeting should not be done by percentages such as bills. Do the remainder of budgeting by the importance of the bills due. Bills are debts that you incur monthly. Bills are the basics. They are the bare minimum of necessities. The goal is to have as few bills as possible. Why? So you can have more mad money to spend - your reward for staying in your budget.

Debt- Debt is a type of bill. It usually means owing something to someone. The term debt is most often referring to a bill that is more than you can pay off in a month. It is most often called a loan. It is not usually the electric bill which is a monthly service. In most situations, you pay debt off over an allotted time.

A widow in the Bible owed money and she almost lost her two sons to slavery. 2 Kings 4:1-7

Money Verse- "Owe no man any thing, but to love one another: for he that loveth another hath fulfilled the law." Romans 13:8

- This verse is referring to bad debt where you did not buy a true asset.

- "I owe, I owe so off to work I go." This is the general thought. I owe, therefore, I must slowly pay off this horrible debt with my meager income that I earn from working three jobs!

- Let me state it this way. Debt can easily be called a liability. Technically, what you bought would be the liability. For the sake of the argument, however, we will call debt a liability.

- The opposite of a liability is an asset.

- You need the opposite of debt! You need assets!

- You do not need a better job with more money! You need assets!

- I hate "Bad Debt." "Bad Debt" is a monster that will eat you alive. It is a very, very appealing monster. Be warned. It is deadly.

- I hope in the future you will tell stories to your children around the campfire about how you defeated the horrible monster "Bad Debt." A truly scary tale!

- "Bad Debt" means you used debt to buy a liability. You need to get rid of this as soon as possible. Debt can be good only if you use it to buy an asset to make more income than the asset costs you in interest, fees, and principle (in both monthly and total payments.) Even still, be extremely cautious when doing this.

Some Types of Debt Are: - Mortgages- when you add up all the interest you pay for your house, you pay three times the purchase price of your house. Should you decide to sell it, then, you sell it for close to what you paid. I do not think that is too smart. Then, your house has to be kept up with different maintenance costs. Yes, a mortgage is a liability.

- However, renting and leasing are worse liabilities.

- If you can buy an older house I would advise it. If you are worried about unexpected surprises, call an inspector. If he/she misses something major, you can sue the inspector and win with all likelihood. If you are a little handy you may want to buy a fixer upper. Sometimes, it pays to call a professional, but, be careful. They may be expensive. Always get an estimate. Sometimes, a few phone calls later, you can have a nice house for much less than you would pay for a new one.

- Car loans are similar to house loans. That shiny new car is probably not worth it simply because it does not produce income. It produces expense.

- Now, of course, there are landlords and cab companies who make money off of cars and houses, but, on the whole they are not worth buying new.

- Credit card debt- I get cold chills. That tiny plastic card should be surgically removed from your hand, your wallet, and your life. Stop spending on a credit card (charge plate) now, now, now, now and oh yes, now.

- Hospital debt - this is a touchy subject, but, hospital bills can be very expensive. I do suggest insurance. How much is up to the individual family.

Money Verse- "He that is surety for a stranger shall smart for it: and he that hateth suretiship is sure." Proverbs 11: 15

Cosigning - Do not cosign. If the person is not trustworthy enough to pay their bills you will get stuck with the bill. You will legally be responsible for the bill.

Money Verse- "Say not unto thy neighbour, Go, and come again, and to morrow I will give; when thou hast it by thee." Proverbs 3:28

I believe this is a command to pay your debts. You need to be honest and pay your debts. This is not an option, but a commandment.

Paying off Debt- Total up the amount of debt that you have. Find out the total amount if you pay only the minimum amount on your debts. This is the amount that you will put into your budget. Set aside a certain amount that you can afford over and above the minimum payments. You can always add to this later. Calculate and find out which bill has the highest interest rate and pay it off first. Do not forget to take the different types of interest into account, so do the math.

Interest - There are two types of interest. The first is simple interest. Simple interest is when you purchase an item and borrow the money. Then the creditor charges you interest on the whole amount - once. You then pay the principle and the interest once.

- The second type is compound interest. Compound interest is when you purchase an item and borrow the money, then the creditor charges you interest on the whole amount for that month. You then pay the principle of a few dollars depending on your loan. However the next month they charge you the interest on the principle again and you pay a little bit of the principle. The next month you do the same thing over again until you slowly pay off this horrible debt. This seems to me to be highway robbery.

Chapter

12

The Budget and Mad Money

Money Story- I have had the good fortune at times to have some mad money. One particular time I remember, I didn't spend it on an exotic vacation. I bought items I could use a lot. I bought a laptop and a GPS. Mad money spends just like regular money – very quickly.

Money Verse –"The blessing of the LORD, it maketh rich, and he addeth no sorrow with it." Proverbs 10:22

Lesson Learned- Buy something with your mad money that you can enjoy over and over, but, buy what you really want with this money.

Mad Money – The amount of money that you have left over after you have fulfilled all other parts of the budget. Money that you can spend without worrying about your conscience. You can spend this however you want to. It is your reward for keeping your budget. Do not feel guilty having fun with this money. Do not be discouraged if it is not a lot at first. It can be very discouraging if you have no mad money to spend. Your investments should help this to grow. But, this is where the money for a new whatever should come from.

Offering- An offering is a love gift to God. You may wish to give a small amount. You may wish to give a larger amount. You should give something in this category. It should be above and beyond the regular 10% tithe (Chapter 2: The Budget and Giving). You may not have a lot of money for this category. This is not a set amount. It is based on how much you wish to give. If you have recently gotten an answer to prayer you may want to add something extra as a thank you for what God has done for you.

Chapter

13

A Pattern to Live By

Money Story- When I was younger, I would, sometimes, sew my own clothes. I bought a pattern from the store. I made many dresses out of that same pattern. It worked great every time. Later, I designed my own dress. The first dress I sewed was great, until I tried to make a second one. It did not turn out so well.

Lesson Learned - When you use the Bible's pattern for success, you always come out with success. When you go your own way, it may work out for a while, but, ultimately, you will fail.

Money Verse-"My son forget not my law; but let thine heart keep my commandments: for length of days, and long life, and peace, shall they add to thee." Proverbs 3:1,2

- Here are some examples of budgets and investments. Please understand they can be adjusted for your needs.

Example:

- Mortimer has a full time job. He works for XYZ Sewage Company. His job really stinks, but it pays the bills. His take home pay is $556/wk. before taxes. There are 4 1/3wks in the average month so he makes approximately $2,409.14/month before taxes (Hint: Use a calculator to do your own budget.)

He starts out the month with a gross of $2,409.14

Now he has to take out his ten percent for giving that is -$240.91

He now has $2,168.23

Now subtract his ten percent savings

from the gross. . . . .-$240.90

He now has $1,927.32

Now subtract ten percent for investing . . . . -$240.91

Total $1,686.41

Taxes (consult a tax professional for your tax rate). . . . . -$200.00

He now has to pay the bills with. $1,486.41

His most important bills get paid first. This may differ from person to person and it is a matter of discretion.

Let's say he views food first . . . . -$320.00

Next his debts:

Mortgage (minimum payment) . . . . -$550.00

He has a 30yr fixed loan at 6% interest

Car payment (minimum payment) . . . .-$50.00

He has a loan for 5 yr. 9% interest

Plus, his extra money for his highest interest loan

(the car loan is the higher interest loan). . . . .-$100.00

Then his other necessities:

Insurance . . . .-$25.00

Gas . . . .-$140.00

Utilities . . . . -$45.00

After bills he has $256.41

So, he has how much mad money? $256.41

- So, he can pay for all the basics, but what if he wants a boat, or a cell phone, or day care for his kids, or private school, etc.? Does he have to get a second job? Does his wife have to work so he can have nice things and smart kids? Read on.

- Now let's say that Mortimer bought a Soda Pop machine with his investment money. He paid $210.00. He sells his pop for $1.50. He pays .60 cents for each one when he buys them in bulk from the supermarket. He still has $30.91. So, he buys 50 for $30.00. Things go well. He sells out in the first week. He has made a gross of $75.00. Take away the cost of $30.00 and he clears $45.00. This goes back into more pop, until the end of the month. Then, he puts the money back into the budget. Now he has more to invest this month because he earned $45.00 a week with his investment. He now has an asset of $195.00 (4 1/3wks.). Not what he paid for the machine ($210.00), but, how much he now makes from the sale of soda pop. This goes into the budget.

Money from job $2,409.14

Money from asset . . . .+ $195.00

He now has $2,604.14

So he takes out his 10% giving . . . . - $260.41

He now has-. $2,343.73

Next he takes out his 10% savings . . . . -$260.41

He now has $2,083.32

Next he takes out his 10% investments . . . . -$260.41

He now has more money for everything. $1,822.91

Now taxes (once again, consult a tax professional) . . . . -$225.00

If his bills have stayed the same he has an extra $111.50

This could be done perpetually. In one year he could easily raise his salary well over (before taxes). $15,230.00

This is significant. Does his wife have to work? Nope.

($2,340+$2,145+$1,950+$1,775+$1,560+$1,365+$1,170 +$975+$780+$585+$390+$195. He, now, has twelve machines. The first machine he bought has sold soda pop for twelve months at $195/month = $2,340.00. The second one has sold for eleven months and so on.)

- He decides he can pay someone to refill them for $20.00/wk. We have not even taken into account the money that has been reinvested. This doubles his investment money every ten months. So then, every ten months a person could add another pop machine to his acquisitions. A person should open an account for their excess investment money, but, do not let this accumulate for long. Get it out there and reinvested.

Chapter
14
Bankruptcy and Individuals

Money Story- The hobo of the Great Depression could tell you a lot about bankruptcy. They would leave their wives and families and go from city to city riding the rails. They hoped that someone would take pity on their families and give them charity. Sometimes, they left in search of work. The men, who stayed with their families, went to government provided soup lines. A relative of mine, who was alive at that time, stood in the soup lines for hours. When he got to the food he would take it home. Then, he would go back and get in line again. After the Depression, to the day he died, he always had cans of food under his bed.

Lesson Learned- My relative was not wrong to do this. He was wise. He, also, followed the ant's example. He worked hard for the rest of his life. Know how to work hard. There is something to working smarter and not harder. Yet, you should know how to work hard. You should have good character yourself. You should not be afraid of hard work.
- A lazy person will be bankrupt simply because he will not work or do anything that resembles work (like operating a business.)

Money Verses - "Slothfulness casteth into a deep sleep; and an idle soul shall suffer hunger." Proverbs 19:15

There are other types of bankrupt individuals.
1.   **Bankrupt People**- Here are four types of bankrupt people:

•   **Ill People (hospital bills)** - The first thing to do is buy medical insurance if you can afford it. Remember you do need some liabilities. Once you have insurance you need to start paying off medical debt. (What better way to do that than assets?)You may feel that you are buried in debt, yet, do not despair. If you let it bother you, some hospital bills may cause discouragement.

- **Loss of Income**- This is a difficult time in a person's life. Take stock of what you do have. You need a wise mentor during this time in your life. Someone who has been where you are.

Job loss - Some people have been devastated by a lost job. Many people have decided to start their business because of a job loss. Sometimes, the difference between a success and a failure is just their attitudes. You should plan ahead for possible job loss.

- **People with a Vice**- You have to kick the habit. You need to protect yourself from temptation. Stay away from the vice. Then completely forget about the vice that had you prisoner. If you need help don't be afraid to ask a professional.

- **Over-spenders**
- What is an over-spender? An over-spender is someone who has a job or income (yes, even assets), but, has too many bills and too much debt. How much is too much? If you cannot even pay the interest on your debt, because you spend too much, you are an over-spender. If you have no money after bills, you are an over-spender. Payday comes and the money is "burning a hole in your pocket"

- Don't be offended. The over-spender is very common. The solution is not always to cut back. It simply may be you need to redirect your shopper's instinct. It can be a good thing to have this instinct if you are shopping for assets. Be aware you need to have a shopper's instinct when it comes to looking for asset investments. Everything you do when shopping for consumables, you also do when shopping for assets. You must consider that you are going to have to spend time buying assets with every paycheck. It helps if you like shopping around and getting a good price. An over-spender can make the best asset investor.

- Some people will never have enough income and should start being accountable to someone. A mentor is an excellent idea. They may need to help you when it comes to your bills. You may think your mentor is a wild, ignorant savage. "My mentor is slashing my "necessities" that I cannot "live without." You probably have a good mentor. This is the best way to overcome overspending habits.

- Another way is to use the envelope trick. Simply place the budget in envelopes marked with each category. Be reasonable. Only spend the money for what it was intended except in an emergency. Another way is to set goals for yourself, little goals at first then bigger goals. Set a time limit on all your goals. Protect yourself from advertisements if they are your downfall. When you do something right, give yourself a small reward. Remember you have to live with you.

Chapter
15
Impulse Shopping

Money Story- Most gas stations do not make their money selling gas. They make their money selling junk food. Look around you at the next gas station you shop at. Does the person ahead of you have junk food in their hand?

Lesson Learned- The products that sell the most at the department stores are the products that are displayed at eye level. You need to build up a resistance to impulse shopping. Bring snacks and refreshments for the trip from a regular store where they are cheaper. Either that or pay for your gas outside. Before you buy anything think. Do I really need it? Obviously you need food, housing, and some form of transportation, but that should be decided at home, not at the store. You should even decide how much you want to spend on an item before you head to the store. If it is not immediately necessary you may want to shop around for a while.

Money Verses- "Love not the world, neither the things that are in the world. If any man love the world, the love of the father is not in him. For all that is in the world, the lust of the flesh, and the <u>lust of the eyes</u>, and the pride of life, is not of the Father, but is of the world. And the world passeth away, and the lusts thereof: but he that doeth the will of God abideth forever." I John 2:15-17 (Note: my underline)

"He becometh poor that dealeth with a slack hand: but the hand of the diligent maketh rich." Proverbs 10:4

"Mine eye affecteth mine heart..." Lamentations 3:51a

Impulse Shopping- This is a big deal. It can happen anywhere. On the television, advertisements proclaim the easy, cheap, liability item that YOU MUST HAVE for only 3 payments of $19.95 plus shipping and handling. But wait there's more. If you buy it within the next 10 minutes you get an additional liability for free! Does this sound familiar? Perhaps, you are at the supermarket and are checking out at the register. You look over and see a magazine with all the latest gossip about your favorite movie star. It is so tempting. Your child (if you have one) sees a candy bar that he or she MUST have. The child will probably throw a tantrum until the child receives either correction or the candy bar. Be aware that the "whatever" is advertising its weakest point. Do not look at billboards on the roadway. Watch where you are going. It's safer, too. The internet is particularly advertisement filled.

Grocery Store- This is difficult because everybody needs to buy food. Don't go in a supermarket hungry. You should always shop from a list. It will help you remember what you need and will keep you from buying impulse items. Do not deviate from your list. If you can, buy in bulk when it is on sale. Try a sample of a new brand to see if you like it before you buy a lot of it. Only buy what you will actually use. Coupons can be a way to go but they take up a lot of time, and, they are rarely for what you actually need. Store ads can be a good thing. You should request ads from your grocer. There is usually a free pile of them on the customer service counter. Do not buy a lot of expensive foods. Don't spend more than $28/wk. per person on food. That is $4 a day. It takes a lot of planning to live on this type of budget. It, also, depends a lot on the price of food in your area. I expect these numbers will become obsolete in the near future. Still be wise in shopping. Do not buy all the rich foods (salty, sugary, and fatty). You may avoid many different health issues.

Chapter
16
It's an Emergency!

Money Story- In 1999, there was a big scare over the dating system of computers. Almost all computers were supposed to crash on December 31st at midnight. Long story short, the expected catastrophe did not occur because of a lot of hard work.

Lesson Learned- There are real emergencies. Prepare for those.

It's an Emergency- Make sure it truly is an emergency. Just because you love that scarf (it is gorgeous) does not make it an emergency. You may not need that tool chest with all those convenient little drawers. Most liabilities can be found in a yard sale in a few months or less.

Money Verse-"Be not afraid of sudden fear, neither of the desolation of the wicked, when it cometh. For the LORD shall be thy confidence, and shall keep thy foot from being taken." Proverb 3:25, 26

- You should have a small amount of cash hidden somewhere easily accessible. Not much of course – just an emergency stash. Also, it would be wise to have a little food and fuel on hand in case of a real emergency.

- Many times when people are just starting out they do not have the things their parents have. They want them now. Their parents have those "things" only after working their whole lives to get those things. Do not be discouraged if you do not have all the nice things your relatives, your neighbors, or your coworkers have. They may have borrowed for it. The grass may be greener on the other side of the fence but it may be artificial turf or you may not want their water bill. Even if they did not borrow for it, keep your focus off of other people's possessions. "Thou shalt not covet." Ask God daily for what you need. Trust him for everything.

Chapter
17
Bankrupt Companies

Money Story- A company many of you would know if I said its name went bankrupt. It was what you would call operating in bankruptcy. The company has come back, somewhat, but, it is a shell of its former self.

Lesson Learned- A bankrupt company can be brought back, but, it is a formidable task.

Money Verses- "The soul of the sluggard desireth, and hath nothing; but the soul of the diligent shall be made fat." Proverbs 13:4

Bankrupt Companies- It is relatively easy to buy a bankrupt company. Sometimes you pay a penny, and, it's yours. However, you now owe all the debt the former owner of the company incurred with the company.

Sometimes, the company may owe less than the company is actually worth. If you sell all the companies commodities you may be in the black. I call that cannibalizing a company. This could also be called corporate raiding.

- Another reason you may buy a bankrupt company is that the former owner may have had a good idea, but was inept at running a company. This is the most common reason for bankruptcy. This type of company can be resurrected but you will need a lot of cash to revive it. Some companies are worth it; others are not. Be warned; this type of deal is risky.

Chapter

18

Why Start a Business?

Or

Business and Generating Income through Investments

Money Story- Betty Business through no fault of her own has just lost her job. Betty sees an opportunity in her area. They have no laundry mat. Since Betty has some savings and investment money already saved she opens a laundry mat. She has only to service her appliances and collect her money.

Lesson learned – Look for a need in your town. If you can fill a need in your town or community you may stand to make a profit.

Money Verse - "No man can serve two masters: for either he will hate the one, and love the other; or else he will hold to the one, and despise the other. Ye cannot serve God and mammon." Matthew 6:24

- Many interpret this verse to mean you should not have money because that means you are serving money; however, in the long run someone with money (even working from the ground up) probably spends less time earning money than someone who works at a job. You should be a master of your money not a slave to it.

Wage Slave- A wage slave could be defined as someone who works for an employer for a specific amount an hour regardless of their profitability. It could also be a salaried worker. Technically, it is not an employee that works on commission. As a wage slave you have very limited things you can do to raise your wage. College is one way to raise your expected wage. Many parents send their kids to college, so their children can get a better job working for some boss. Why is that the extent of their dreams for their children?! It is probably the notion that they have inherited from their parents. Some minds are trapped in the notion that working a job is all there is in the world. It is the only thing that is legal and safe in their minds. I realize that the term "Wage Slave" is very strong. It is only used to try to get your attention and shake up the notion that you have to have a job!

Plan and Time Your Escape to Freedom - If you have a job you may not want to immediately quit. Use your job to be a spring board to a better life.

Money Story- When I was little we had chickens. I took care of them for my family, In truth, the chickens ate more money in feed than we actually would have paid for the eggs at the store. All I had to do was give them water, food, and let them outside for a while. I did a lot of thinking in that barn.

Lesson Learned- Even if you don't make a profit you will learn a lot.

Money Verse - "In all labour there is profit: but the talk of the lips tendeth only to penury." Proverbs 14:13

Businesses Can Be Three Basic Types

- **Self Employed Business**- You have to go into work every day to manage or in some way watch over your business.

- **Owner/Employee**- You do not have to worry about your business. You have hired right and trained right, so you simply cash in your check.

For example, John works at a tire shop. He sells tires. His boss pays him $9.00/hr. He sells 8 tires a week on average for a total of $800/wk. He makes his boss $400.00 profit. Is he a good employee? John makes $360.00 gross. Yes. He is worth his pay. He makes less than he sells. Every boss in the world would like to hire John.

Also, you have to have your business on a budget, just like your personal life. Remember the story of the talents and the servants. Our Lord expects a return on investment. It is not greediness to invest and expect a return on your investment.

- **Partnership**- A true partnership is 50% for you and 50% for your partner. A person that has 51% or more controls the business. Many businesses have failed because of poor partnerships. I do not prefer partnerships.

Chapter

19

If at First You Don't Succeed Don't Try Sky Diving!

Or

Starting Your First Business

Money Story - This is best illustrated by a child (the owner) selling lemonade (the product). The child is meeting a need (the demand). It is hot outside. People are thirsty (his customer). He sells lemonade on the corner (his location), so, he can make some money (his profit). Many times, the mother (his supplier) will give the child the lemonade. If he had to pay for the lemonade (his cost) he probably would not make a profit his first time unless he has help from an adult (his mentor).

Lesson Learned- You will probably need help your first time, too. Though, once you learn, you will probably not forget.

Money Verse- Seest thou a man diligent in his business? He shall stand before kings; he shall not stand before mean men." Proverbs 22:29

Starting a Business - This is the first of three ways to get a business.

- Many times you grow with the business. You learn about people and life. Never sell more than 49% share of your business when you are starting out.

It All Starts with an Idea - An engine will not run without a spark. Your first idea for a new business may not be that great, but, it might be that spark. Ask your mentor about it anyway. You mentor may see potential that you do not see. He or she may modify your idea and make it usable. The Chinese proverb is give a man a fish feed him for a day. Teach a man to fish feed him for a life time. You only have to learn how to fish once. You will probably only have to learn how to run a business once. It all starts with a spark. That first spark in the engine of your mind is priceless.

Start Small - Do not get in too deep at first until you are confident at what you are doing, especially, if you are borrowing money to start your business.

Start With What You Know- If you know nothing about a specific business, do not go into that business starting out. You need to use your experience in a particular field to your advantage. When you have experience in your field, you give yourself a boost above others. Then, when you have succeeded in what you do know and gained more experience, you can move on to bigger and better things. Always go into any business with a teachable attitude. Learn everything you can. When you invest in what you know, you could save yourself much grief. If you know a certain area well it may be wise to stick to it. It is not wrong to venture outside your comfort zone. Do not let inexperience be a constrictor. Constantly expand your horizons. But, before you take a leap of faith, look where you're going. In other words learn something about what you are going to invest in. When investing on the job training is costly and time consuming.

Litigation- Be careful when starting your business. You may wish to consult your attorney. You may want to consult your attorney before you take your product to market. The added expense of consulting an attorney may save you money in the long run.

When Starting the Business- Make sure you form your business under the correct type of corporation for your business. I suggest you get an attorney for this and have the attorney explain all your options. Also, consult your mentor. This is not a step you will want to skip.
- When you start a business make sure there is room for expansion. Also, make sure you can take on the competition.

Competition- Obviously, the less competition you have the better. You should research the competition before starting out. You may not want to get into a business that has too much competition. Also, you may not want to go into a business that can be easily copied or that is not original.

Don't Follow Failure - If most people cannot succeed in a particular industry do not get into that industry yourself. For instance, I do not get into the restaurant business. I would not even if I could cook well, which I cannot. Why? Because of the many, many people who have failed.

Do Not Let Fear Cripple You- If you start deciding never to do something because of fear, you will soon do nothing at all. I am not talking about doing stupid things that will hurt you. I am talking about not doing something because of presumed failure before you even start.

Watch Out for Theft- Shoplifting is a major concern. You will have to factor that into your business plan. Employee theft is also a huge problem. Be aware of the danger.

-Not just shoplifting is a concern. I hate the thought, but someone may steal your first idea. Do not stop thinking. Do not get a chip on your shoulder and give up. Continue to expand your mind. Do not steal anyone else's idea. To steal an idea is both illegal and immoral. Make sure your mentor is on your side and does not unnecessarily talk about your idea with someone else or steal your idea for himself. You may wish to consider some type of licensing or patent which may not be cheap!

Chapter

20

Buying a Business

Money Story- Simple Simon is buying a business. He decides to buy an ice cream shop. He has never run a company before. He thinks the former owner, Smart Sally, was not very good at running a business. So, he decides to make huge changes to the business. He thinks he can increase his profit by firing a few employees. He expects he will not have any competition in the winter. So, he closes down his summer operations. He will soon have to close because he miscalculated.

Lesson Learned- Sometimes taking short cuts can hamper your business.

Money Verse- "Again, the kingdom of heaven is like unto a merchant man, seeking goodly pearls: Who, when he had found one pearl of great price went and sold all that he had, and bought it." Matthew 13:45

Buying a Business- Look for a company that you can grow. This is a little bit harder, but, it is not impossible. Simple companies are easy to run. They are also easy to copy, so be careful, you may have competition on your hands. Shop around. Learn all you can from the former owner. Find out if the employees are fiercely loyal or if they will work for you, as well. Learn all you can about your soon to be new employees. Find out their habits and character, their likes and dislikes, also, who you will have to fire (do not disclose this before you buy the business). Find out what the business owns, the clientele (customers), and how it operates. You need to weigh the price of the business and the debt of the business, against the profit margin of the business. This is called the price/earnings ratio. That is – how many years it would take to pay off the company if earnings remained the same. The lower this number is, the more desirable the company.

The Franchise- The franchise is an easy way to buy a business. It is usually not cheap. It is not fool proof. "Nothing is fool proof to a sufficiently talented fool."

Chapter

21

Inheriting a business

Money Story- Our friend Simple Simon is in trouble again. His Father Papa Pete has just died. He left him his business. Simple Simon has no experience. He does not like his father's employees, so he fires them. However, he has no idea how to run a business. He has just fired the only people who do. What do you think will happen to Simple Simon's business?

Lesson Learned- This may be the hardest of all. Especially, if the person you inherit it from has not taught you about their business, or made plans for you to run it.

Money Verse- "He that gathereth in the summer is a wise son: but he that sleepeth in harvest is a son that causeth shame." Proverbs 10:5

Most fathers in the Bible left their farm to their sons. This was their inheritance. As you can see they were expected to keep it up and care for it.

Money Verse- "He that troubleth his own house shall inherit the wind: and the fool shall be servant to the wise of heart." Proverbs 11:29

Inheriting a Business- If your family has never taught you about a business, you are going to need to cram like you have a test tomorrow. Read books if you can, but, your biggest tutors are going to be your employees.

Chapter

22

Most Rich People shop at Discount Retailers

or

Running the Business as the Business Owner – You

Perception - Again, many think that when you're rich, you have to live like you're rich. You have to have the nice clothes, nice cars, and fancy houses or anything else that defines you as rich. A very damaging stereotype of rich people is that they all buy expensive things and waste their money in general. Many people think that rich people are lazy. Nothing could be more wrong. Many rich people work harder than most other people. They also shop at discount retailers and find bargains most people overlook because most other people are too busy! They understand that if you don't spend it you will have it!

Money Story- Simple Simon is so stuck on himself that he doesn't realize he needs help with his business. He thinks he is as smart, lucky, and charming as he can possibly be. He has a horrible temper and he also cusses regularly. He has no idea why his employees quit. He never gives raises or thinks about anyone but himself. His business is in a downward spiral.

Lesson Learned- You can change your attitude. You can learn how to run a business right. You just have to admit you're wrong in some areas. You must find in yourself a teachable attitude.

Get a Mentor- Good advice can save you much grief. Bad advice can cost you an infinite amount of money. Be careful who you trust, but, trust someone. The more wise people that you ask the better.

Money Verse -"Where no counsel is, the people fall: but in the multitude of counselors there is safety." Proverbs 11:14

A Mentor - You are becoming who your friends are. A mentor will say "I have faith in you" even when you think you will fail. A mentor will help you set goals in your life. They will be there to celebrate when you reach those goals. They will be "a shoulder to cry on" if you fail. Always, select a mentor who has been where you are and is now where you want to be. Select a mentor who will take you under his or her "wing". "In a multitude of counselors there is safety."

Make Friends - The more people that you know the better. If you are shy set a goal for yourself of meeting one new person a week. Then keep that goal. When mom said "Don't talk to strangers." she didn't mean when you become an adult. A good friend can be a blessing. A new friend can expand your mind. Everyone knows something I do not know.

Money Verse - "And I say unto you, Make to yourselves friends of the mammon of unrighteousness; that when ye fail, they may receive you into everlasting habitations." Luke 16:9

Do Not Put Too Much Faith in People - Everyone will disappoint you at some time, except Jesus Christ. You should still trust people. You should be able to tell your employees "I have faith in you." and not be lying.

A Doer - Be a doer not a talker. Do not be the type of person that just sits around and talks but never does anything. Especially, when you are supposed to be obeying something God has told you to do in His Word.

Money Verse - "But be ye doers of the word, and not hearers only, deceiving your own selves." James 1:22

Goals- Many books have been written on this subject. Most people are goal oriented. That is they preform better when given a goal to shoot for (usually with a reward). If this is you, you need to set goals for yourself – a big goal or small steps - whatever works for you. Remember, business is often not about aptitude but about tenacity. They are many people who are successful in business that cannot even read!

Education - I am for education. I am not for borrowing for education. Go to a community college if that's all you can afford. If you go to college and work at the same time you may want a lighter college credit load. It may take you a little longer, but it will be worth it. Also, it will be the same degree whether you get it there, or at a big name college. If your parents have scrimped and saved for you to go to college at a big name school – great. When you start making money, remember your parents with repayment. It's okay if it's more than they gave you.

Retirement- Most people think that you need to save a large amount of money for retirement. It does not hurt, but it is not necessary. You need assets for retirement that are generating income. You may wish to save for retirement if your assets fail.

Double Your Money - If you had the option to choose between A. $1,000 a day for 60 days or B. a penny that doubles every day for 60 days. - Which would you take? If you said, "A" you would have $60,000. If you said "B" you would have $5,764,607,523,034,234.88 (If my addition is right. My calculator doesn't go that high.). My point is that you need to do calculations before you make a decision. Don't assume anything. That is how fortunes are lost (please note: this is not an offer).

The Lottery - The lottery is a tax on people who are bad at math. In other words, do not participate in the lottery. This includes scratch offs. You have a better chance of being struck by lightning than winning the lottery. Do not depend on "winning" for your retirement.

Sleep - When you go to bed, ask Christ to wake you when you need to get up. Ask him to help you get quality sleep. Also, the only thing you should do in bed is sleep.

- Another problem many people fall prey to is that they do not get enough sleep and others get too much sleep. You truly need your eight hours.

Money Verse - "How long wilt thou sleep, O sluggard? When wilt thou arise out of thy sleep." Proverbs 6:9

- This person is getting too much sleep.

Money Verse - "It is vain for you to rise up early, to sit up late, to eat the bread of sorrows: for so he giveth his beloved sleep." Psalms 127:2

This person gets too little sleep.

The Danger Zone - This person thinks he or she must work very hard for their business to succeed. They think that they must do everything themselves. As you can see they have limits. They think they are lazy if they don't do all the work and simply cannot afford to hire anyone.

- This is the danger zone. Many, many people are TRAPPED here. This occurs when a person is not willing to hire help. They do too much of the foot work. They get worn out doing all the grunt work. They do not realize when they <u>add</u> an employee that they <u>multiply</u> the amount of work that gets done. A <u>good</u> employee may work harder for you than you will for yourself.
- If you cannot afford to hire someone to take your place and still make a profit you should reconsider your business. You do not have an asset until you can afford to pay decent wages, and still make a profit. You should be able to sit back and watch the first business grow while starting a new, second business, etc. This will increase your bottom line exponentially.

Appearance - You should dress for the impression you want to give. You may want to look rich. Perfume, cologne, jewelry, deodorant, make up, hair, all contribute to your impression. There are many books for this. There are even people called image consultants that do this for a living. You may want a professional opinion. You may **not** want to look rich. In that case, do not dress in designer clothing. Many people judge you by your clothes, hygiene, accent, and other factors.

Chapter
23
Running the Business and the Employee

Money Story - I have worked with a lot of different people. I have in mind one particular person. He would walk around looking lost. He did not know what to do at all. The problem was he was never trained. After a few days, he gave up and quit.

Lesson Learned- An employee, who is untrained, will quit if you do not train him. Even if all he does is sit around, he will quit.

Selecting an Employee - You need to make a list of the things most important to you in an employee. No one can do this for you. A mentor may help you and guide you, but, ultimately the decision is yours to make. Their personality, character, hygiene, are things you have to consider when hiring new employees.

Learn People- Study their character and personality. This is the most important thing. Learn this lesson and with a little hard work, you can achieve almost anything in life. The people that make the most money in this world are the people who know people.
1. The more you know about people's character the easier the job of managing your employees will be.
2. The more you know about people's personality the easier it will be to solve disagreements.
3. The more you know about what people want the more you know what people will buy.

The Appearance - To uniform, or not to uniform. This is another judgment call. You may need to supply your employees with their uniforms or make them cheap enough, so, your employees can easily afford them. Most employees are happier in their own clothes and jewelry. If at all possible, let them wear what they want. Should you decide to uniform, make sure your employees get a copy of the rules.

Scheduling- Hire the employee that has the hours and availability you need. Do not plan your schedule too far ahead. The reason is most employees don't plan that far ahead. Things do come up. It is not a question of character. You will lose employees that you have already trained. Training new employees translates into losing money. You have to pay them while they are being trained. Also, allow for absences: Weather, sickness, traffic jams and other things.
- If you need to ask for overtime, make sure it is worth the employee's while. No one wants to spend all their time at work. If you have a busy season, you may have employees who want a graduated payment. They may want their paycheck to stay relatively the same. Still, make sure you give them extra for overtime.

Employees and the Interview - If this is your first interview, you probably will not be prepared for what you are about to experience. May I suggest you write down everything that was said. It will protect you later. I would suggest an approach similar to looking for a babysitter. Character is a must. You may want to rate your potential employees for what you need in filling the position. Appearance, cleanliness, punctuality, honesty, kindness, alertness, and teachability are all a part of character. Education is important but it is not always necessary. Experience is preferable. Wages are important to everyone. You may need to check their ability to sell if that is important to your job vacancy. You can pay in different ways. These ways are commission, contract, salary, hourly, tip. Make sure you can afford the employee.

- The guilt trip is a ploy many people use to get what they want. They may use it in their interview. It may very well be a legitimate concern, but, they try to portray themselves as victims. They try to make you feel guilty telling them "no". They may, then, pout. If you have never seen an adult pout, be prepared. It is not a pretty sight. A temper tantrum, usually, is accompanied by violent anger. They may see you as a rich owner authority figure. They may see you as a bank. They may see you as their best friend. However they see you initially, you need them to see you as boss first and foremost. Do not become romantically involved with your employee. Your employee's vision of you can make or break your relationship. Do not let it break you or your company. Show them the door first.

Beware the Perpetually Disgruntled Employee- He was mad at his last boss, the boss before him, and the boss before him. He will turn traitor on you, too. This type of employee will turn traitor on whoever is in charge. They are never happy with any boss that they have. They sour the atmosphere of the work place. They will probably have a good attitude for a short time after they are hired. This quickly turns to a critical attitude. This is a contagious attitude and a dangerous person. Watch out!

The Manager - A manager does everything you would do as the boss. He hires, fires, supervises, signs paychecks, and makes sure the company runs smoothly.

- A manager needs to be trained in all the areas he or she is over. You may want to make a list of responsibilities for this important person. Teach him his/her job inside and out. Check on this person regularly. You may decide to let this person do first interviews to gain experience. At first, you and this person need to be together for a second interview and hiring. Once this person has experience, you may allow them to hire on their own. A good rule of thumb is to never allow them to hire their friends or relatives. That is a recipe for disaster. It may be a good rule for you, too.

Little is Much- Pay attention to detail. Read the fine print. When hiring someone, look for the little things that will tell you about the person. For instance, a person with dirt under their fingernails may be careless. Or the person may be a hard worker. A mechanic with grease under his/her nails that won't come out may be a hard-worker. A person with rough hands probably works with his hands.

Money Verse - "He that is faithful in that which is least is faithful also in much: and he that is unjust in the least is unjust also in much." Luke 16:10

Lesson Learned- There is NO such thing as a little white lie. It is a big, dirty lie.

Illegal Immigrants - If the immigrant is not willing to keep the law, and go through the process of becoming a legal citizen, do you think that they will bother to keep your rules as a business owner? Also, for you to break the law and hire them is not a good reflection on your character. You may feel that it is a humanitarian question because you want to help the poor. Should you decide to do this you are honor bond, in my opinion, to help them to become a citizen.

Hiring- This is when you tell the person what he or she is going to make. You must pay minimum wage, also, do not rip anyone off. If they are worth more, be honest. Pay more.

- Please note you do not have to hire anyone who does not have the credentials, who does not interview well, or who you cannot get along with. You should in no way be racist, bigoted or gender discriminatory.

The Trainee - Train, train, train. If you have to err – over-train. Make a science of it. Take the guesswork out of the job. Measure amounts. Teach the employee exactly what they are to do.

Training- Do not expect your employees to understand their job without extensive training. If his job is simply to push a button, explain what is happening inside the machine. When the machine breaks down, he will understand when to stop pushing the button.

- An employee might be late for work. Do not swear at this employee. Do not immediately fire this employee. Calm down, and then make the decision. Be an adult. Do not let anger get in the way of your success.

- Ultimately, you must train your workers well. Undertrained or poorly trained workers are a liability. It is not their fault. Do not fire an undertrained employee. He is undertrained because of you.

Enthusiasm- Most of the time, an employee will work for you better than you will work for yourself. If you are not sure you can afford an employee, simply save up two weeks of pay. Next, hire an employee with the understanding that unless the company makes a large enough profit, they will only be employed for a two week period.

Attitude - This is important. When dealing with the public be over-happy. When you are away from the public and are with your employees, be polite, kind, and firm. If you have to yell to get your point across, someone needs to be let go. Your employees need to respect each other and each other's privacy. You may decide that work is no place for establishing romantic relationships. In no case should you have a romantic relationship with an employee. Also, no advancement should be made based on romantic relationships. This should be enforced by loss of job with both parties involved.

Gratitude- This is crucial. It is one of the greatest "secrets" of business. Unwisely thank you is often left out of our lives. True gratitude is forgotten. This should not be. Your mother probably taught you to say thank you. She would probably call please and thank you the "magic" words. She is right. Gratitude is an attitude.

The Paycheck

- DO: Pay on time every time.

- DON'T: Pay late, short, or take tips/commissions away from your employees.

The Break and Lunch- Employees must get their breaks and lunches on time every time. Perhaps, stagger the shift times to suit your needs.

The Quarterly Review- This should be a true reflection on what took place. Be fair. Give raises when they are deserved.

The Sales Team- They should be natural salesmen. Teach them the ten word rule.

The Ten Word Rule - A very simple rule is - use no more than ten words at a time. The salesman should speak ten words, and then, let the customer talk as long as they want. Also, answer the customer's questions in ten words or less.

Sales- You should learn sales. This is important. Learn what works for your individual product. Do not necessarily use a pitch. The best pitch is one the customers do not realize is a pitch. Make the options clear. Do not ramble on and on. Explain clearly. Do not act bored. Remember, excitement is contagious.

- Every business needs sales to operate. The heartbeat of any business is sales. You need to learn to sell for yourself, before you start your business. If you are shy, or if you are outgoing the same basic principles apply

- Don't try to confuse them. I have never bought anything that I did not understand how to use. Nor, did I buy a product that I did not know how much it cost after all the payments.

- You should not talk to your customer like he or she is stupid. Yet, you should be able to sell your product to a 2 year old. If you know a two year old, see if he or she would buy your product after listening to your presentation.

- Let the customer talk while you listen. Truly listen. If you do not have the product that they need, be honest, tell them where they can find it.

- This should go without saying, but you should never use swearing, inappropriate, or foul language with a customer or an employee. An angry customer might make you angry. Express your anger like an adult. Whatever you do, do not throw things or punch anyone, unless, you are being physically attacked. Do not throw a temper tantrum.

- Address their concerns. Give simple answers. Do not try to swindle your customer. Happy customers are repeat customers. Do not intimidate your customer. I do not return to a company where I feel intimidated.

The Raise and Promotion- Give raises as your business plan will allow. Allow for them. This is an issue. If an employee has exceeded expectations in making profit for the company, he/she should not have to ask for a raise. You should automatically give the raise. I consider it the honest thing to do. Promotions are a little different. You should always look for the employee that is most suited for the promotion position. Some people prefer simply promoting on seniority, as a matter of principle. If that is you - great. Do not promote based on a romantic relationship. It might be okay to promote or hire based on a friendship. I would do this only if the reason you are promoting/hiring your friend is the friend's character. You may know that your friend has the right personality for the job at hand.

Unions - Unions can be good or evil. Originally, unions were a very good thing. They stopped the horrible working conditions of the manufacturing era. However, they also stopped the manufacturing era. Not right away, of course, but slowly, over time. Now unions cry poor. They destroy a company because they aren't willing to negotiate, and then say that the business owner was too greedy. A union can be a business owner's worst nightmare

Chapter
24
The Business Plan or Making a Battle Strategy

- Why do I call it a battle strategy? Because you will feel like you are going to war!

Money Story- Simple Simon wants to buy a business. He has no idea how much to pay for it. He overpays for the business. He has no idea what he is doing. He, also, overpays for his goods. He never advertises his business or gives his workers a raise. He has no idea if he is making money or not. How long do you think he will be in business because he has no business model?

Lesson Learned- The first thing to do is add up your expenses. Then, see how much product or services you would have to sell before you would turn a profit. Does that seem to be a reasonable goal number? The business plan should be done before you start or buy a business. These need to be real numbers. Do not guess at these numbers. Every tiny detail needs to be taken into account: Rent, taxes, insurance, manufacturing cost, advertising, payroll, legal fees, maid service, cleaning supplies and more. Don't forget the toilet paper! There are many things to think about. Do not forget anything. You have to make a profit. You need a profit at the end of the **first day**. Do not lose sight of this - **ever**. If your income is more than your outgo you will succeed. If it's not, you will have to raise your prices. If the market won't pay it you are out of business. Sometimes, if the problem is production cost you can lower your prices and sell more by making a larger amount of your product for less. I would probably not do this starting out because you may get stuck with the inventory.

Money Verse - "Or what king, going to make war against another king, sitteth not down first, and consulteth whether he be able with ten thousand to meet him that cometh against him with twenty thousand." Luke 14:31

Sell It Before You Make it- Sell your product before you make it if at all possible. This is sometimes called a purchase order. You may wish to start taking actual money and actual orders. You may wish to simply take an order. Sometimes, you may want a deposit that the customer will lose if they back out of the deal. If you do any of these ways, you will need to let your customer know there will be a waiting period for the product. If your customer is a major retailer this may be the easiest way to go. This sounds weird to most people. Most people who are starting a new product, start with manufacturing their new product. They pour their heart, soul, and last dollar into making their new product. They then have pallets of new material made(if they make it that far) that they cannot sell(most of the time) because the company buying the product wants to change it in some way. They do not have the money to make these changes and they have a lot of worthless product on their hands. It seems to be the biggest mistake new business people make in my opinion, when manufacturing, because they should be selling their product **before** they manufacture it. You may want to patent it and make a prototype so that you will have something to show to buyers. You will also have to figure how much it will cost to make it(so in the end you will know how much to charge for it) and how long it will take to make it. I suggest if at all possible you sell your idea to stores as a product long before you ever have a large order of your actual product complete. I find this to be the best way to do this. I understand you wish to put your best foot forward but a prototype will probably take care of that. Make sure your prototype looks like the finished product and also looks professional. You will also find out if your product will sell.

The Ideal Situation- It is possible to have your business plan so that you incur no cost(production, taxes, or otherwise) until you actually make a sale. Upon making a sale you manufacture the product and pay your taxes and everyone else - all less than what your sale price was for. As you can see the advantage is that you will never go out of business because you ran into the red column on your ledger. You may run out of customers, but you will not run into the red.

Investor Friendly-It is much easier to get an investor to help you manufacture your product if you already have an actual order for your product. You may not need an investor if you can pay your manufacturer after your customers pay you.

Patent Pending- You may get away with not having a patent for your product while production is in place, only if you are not infringing on someone else's patent. Be careful! No one wants a lawsuit on their hands!

Oops!- Should the unfortunate happen and your product is manufactured incorrectly you need to have the backbone to insist on quality. I recommend not paying your manufacturer until **your** customer is satisfied! If it is a mistake on your part you will have to eat the cost. Please be clear. Order correctly. A sample may be a good idea.

Taxes, Taxes, Taxes– Plan on paying your taxes. You need to put this cost into your budget long before tax day. This can catch you off guard if you are not ready for it. Especially because you are not having it deducted automatically from your paycheck (You may not be getting a set paycheck when you are in business for yourself.).

 Do not forget to include taxes in your business plan. Do not commit tax fraud. Get the help of a certified public accountant and pay your taxes. They are worth it and if they make an egregious error you can sue. Also, you are likely to win the suit. Do not try bank accounts in other countries or anything shady. Always be above board. You will not regret it. Christ tell us to pay our taxes. (Matthew 22:21)

Keep Your Receipts- This is a must. You will need them to show business expenses for tax deductions. You may need to prove to the insurance company how much you invested in a property should it burn or be destroyed because of flood.

Record Your Mileage- Always record your odometer when you start driving to when you arrive when you take a trip for a business reason.

Insurance- This can be a necessity. A wise mentor can help you know what to buy for your situation. Do not look at the insurance salesman as a wise mentor. He is trying to sell you insurance.

Utilities- Ask the former owner or the landlord to give you an estimate of how much the utilities will normally be per month. Do not waste money leaving lights on that do not need to be on.

Rent or Own- This is big. It may be better to rent when starting at a new location. It may be better to rent when starting a new business. Overall, owning is a better choice in the long run. Buying is a good way to go if you are sure you have selected the right place. Buying with cash is usually preferable. You can be very creative with this aspect of the business (You may just have that bass boat that the seller always wanted.). You may be able to agree to a percentage of your profitability if you decide to rent - whatever you can agree on that is both moral and legal.

Your Business Orientation- Businesses that are family oriented make the most money. Family is the most lucrative word that there is for making money in business.

Chapter
25
The Product

Money Story- Once, I bought a particular product that I did not like. It advertised a heating system, as well as, a massager. It barely heated up. I was not happy with this product.

Lesson Learned- Make sure you deliver what you advertise. Your product needs to be the same thing every time or improved in some way. You would be wise to have some kind of quality control set up. Do not sell inferior merchandise or a poorly inspected product.

Money Verse- "A good name is rather to be chosen than great riches, and loving favour rather than silver or gold." Proverbs 22:1

Fulfill A Need- There are things everyone needs to live. If you are the main supplier of that product you may not have a lot of growth, but your business should be steady.

Solve A Problem -Your product will sell faster if it solves a problem that most people have.

Build A Better Mouse Trap- A product that is an improvement on an already great product may be easy to sell.

Fads- Your product has "must have" appeal. To a certain extent this can be achieved through advertising. Fads that have run their course are hard to sell. Products that are out of date or behind the times are hard to sell.

Keep It Simple Stupid- Your product should be easy to use. The directions should be easy to understand. The simpler it is to use the better.

Brand· This is big. People will recognize your company by its name, symbol, or maybe a little jingle. You want them to think of your product first when they need the particular item that you sell. They will often think of your product whenever they need that kind of item. This could easily be called having mind shares or renting space in your customer's heads.

You want to have a patent on anything that you sell. If you do not, somebody will undercut you. You need to have trade marks on your company name, commercials, and anything that has to do with your brand.

Patent- If you invent a new product you will need to get a patent. Do not sell or give away your product without one(unless you feel you want to run the risk of copyright infringment(on your part or someone else's).

Royalties- Let's say a company decides that they need your patented product to enhance their product. They will offer you a royalty. This can easily be called an asset. However, do not sell yourself short. Make a wise deal.

Your Packaging- This is also important for three reasons. Your packaging should make your product more appealing. Eye catching packaging is a must. Colors matter. Brighter colors will probably sell better.

Your packaging should also provide necessary information about your product. You need to list ingredients without giving away your secret recipe. Any extra credibility you can add to your product should be listed on your packaging.

Your packaging should be child friendly. You do not want a dangerous, poorly made product or packaging on the market. Even if you are not sued and someone gets hurt you will have to live with the guilt the rest of your life.

Timing- If your product is time sensitive you need to make sure your product is "out" at the right time. A swimming pool probably won't sell in January with a foot of snow on the ground.

Safety- Every business has its own unique set of problems. Some businesses need approval from different types of government bureaucracies and agencies before they can sell their product. Safety is a big deal to everyone. You do not want anyone to be injured, hurt or killed because they used your product.

Manufacturing- I prefer all manufacturing be done in the country it is going to be sold in. For some products you will have to make a mold before you can begin production. This can be very expensive. Fortunately, it is a one-time cost.

The Distributor- This is a staple in the "just in time" delivery system. It helps only with bigger businesses. It takes orders from your multiple stores and makes sure the right store gets resupplied with the right product.

Inventory- In the old days, companies had to order large amounts and hope they sold. You may still have to do this but only a little. Remember, you want to sell your product before you make it. You can order exactly as much as you need in most cases.

Advertising- This is a big part of brand. Millions of dollars every year go into catching the public eye. A jingle, a color scheme, a funny commercial - anything can put you above the rest. When advertising on the television, a good simple rule is to change the screen every three seconds.

Door Buster- You may want to consider this. A door buster is an item usually of a limited quantity that you sell drastically below market value on certain date. It is intended to attract new customers to your business and get them in the door. It can be a huge help if the customer gets to see your store in a positive light.

Shipping- Don't forget this cost. Shipping your product can be costly. Try and find the cheapest way to do this. You may want to hire a new employee as a driver and buy a truck or you may want to ship it more traditionally. There are many companies that will do this for a price. Either way make sure you figure out the cost and put it in your business plan.

Chapter
26
Price

Money Story- I love cheap. I love a good deal. When I go to a restaurant, I almost always pick from the dollar menu. I am thinking of a business that went bankrupt because it was known as a low price business. They thought they could attract the rich by raising their prices. This did not work.

Lesson Learned-Perception is a key in pricing. If you are seen as a discount retailer you probably need to stay a discount retailer. If you are known as an upscale store, stay an upscale store.

Money Verse – "It is naught, it is naught, saith the buyer: but when he is gone his way, then he boasteth." Proverbs 20:14

Pricing- This is the most important step. Everything must be considered when determining the price of your product. If you do this wrong you can kiss your company goodbye. Any hidden costs, that you forget to add into the price, will come back to bite you later. You want to keep your production costs low. I repeat. You need a profit at the end of the **first day**.

- Your price must also reflect what the market will bear. Another way of saying this is: What will people pay for your product? You need to make sure your cost is less than your sale price. Do not over-charge your customer.

The Customer- Keep your customer happy. Know your customer. Know your type of customer. This is also called your demographic. Rich, poor, young, old, male, female, you need to know who buys your product. For instance, most children do not need dentures. When buying or starting a company make sure that you have a wide enough demographic to support your company. In other words make a product that everyone wants and needs to buy.

Chapter
27
Brick and Mortar
The Business: Buildings and Land

Money Story- Farmer Full has just noticed that the local grocery store is closing. Farmer Full sees an opportunity. He buys the land under the grocery store. He then rents the building out to a local children's arcade. In the morning before the arcade opens Farmer Full pulls out his fresh fruits and veggies cart. He now has a place to sell his vegetables while his tenant(the arcade) pays the bills for the property.

Lesson Learned- You may have more than one aspect to your business.

Money Verse-"For which of you, intending to build a tower, sitteth not down, and counteth the cost, whether he have sufficient to finish it. Lest haply, after he hath laid the foundation,and is not able to finish it, all that behold it begin to mock him, Saying, This man began to build, and was not able to finish." Luke 14:28-30

Building a New Building- When building a new building **expect** problems. Expect it to cost more to build it than you are quoted.

Decoration and Maintenance- Maintenance is key in a business. You need to keep your buildings up and in good repair. You also need to keep you buildings relatively modern, unless an antique theme is part of the décor. Paint them when they need painted. There are people that can decorate your business for you, if you want a professional opinion. Interior and exterior decorators can help.

Keep It Clean, Neat, and Organized- This is an important part of your business. Most customers prefer a clean business. No one wants to go into a store that smells bad. Also, your items will probably sell faster if a customer can find them easily.

Be Considerate of Your Customers– Restrooms are a nice feature if they are kept clean. A place to sit and rest is also nice. A water fountain that is clean is a plus.

Location, Location, Location- Buy, build, or rent a good location. It can be worth the cost. If you do not have a good location there are a few things you can do.

1.   Focus on internet sales. - Internet business can be profitable. Get a good website. Shipping is a big deal. An internet business has different problems than a brick and mortar business.

2.   Relocate - Relocation can be an easy fix. You just need to find an open shop in a better area. Make sure you can afford it in your business plan.

3.   Advertise - An advertisement can be the cheapest fix. Make sure your location is the central part of the advertisement.

4.   Give up - Many people have failed at business. Sometimes, you just have to cut your losses. You may want to admit defeat. You may want to try a different type of business. A business may not be for you. I hope, however, that is not the case. Should you decide against running your own business, you may invest in someone else's business. Make sure they can run a business while you sit on the sidelines.

Chapter

28

Your Bank Account

Money Story- Simple Simon is back again. He is so excited he just opened his new bank account. He does not record his purchases and in one week he overdrawn and has to pay a late fee.

Lesson Learned- If you have a problem balancing your account you will overdraft on a regular basis. One way is to simply take out the amount you will need for each day from the bank so that there are no atm fines.

Balancing Your Account – Keeping track of every penny is important. You should use a ledger. You can get those at your bank. You simply record the amount of purchase, the date, and if it is credit, debit, or check. Also, if it's a deposit or withdrawal. Then you subtract the amount you spent from your bank balance. Your check number goes in the far left corner. Always respect your budget when making a purchase.

Money Verse - "He also that is slothful in his work is brother to him that is a great waster." Proverbs 18:9

Waste Not Want Not- Try to keep your bills down by turning off lights that you aren't using. Don't run the utilities unnecessarily. Don't get cable or satellite unless you truly can afford it. Give up drinking alcohol, smoking, and illegal drugs if you use them. Don't eat out for every meal. Learn to cook. Learn to read a recipe. The internet has many good recipes.

Cash On Hand – Keep some cash on hand for emergencies, but not too much because your house may be broken into. (Do not tell people you do not trust that you are going on a vacation or won't be home.)

Also, keep track of your cash just like you would your bank account. After they lived through the Great Depression many people did not trust banks. They would keep their money under their mattresses.

Using Your Bank Card: Debit Or Credit - Make sure to record in your ledger when you use your bank card. When you use your card as credit it does not come out of your account immediately. When you use your card as debit, the money comes out of your account immediately. Also, you do not need a credit card to order things off the internet. You can use your bank card.

Using Your Check Book – If you have never written a check before it is a simple process. On the line marked "date" you write the date that you wrote the check. By the next line that says "pay to the order of" you write who the check is for. Underneath that line you fill in the amount the check is for. You must spell out the words. For example: One hundred thirty four dollars. At the end of the line you write the change in numbers above a line that has 100 underneath it. This line has the word dollar at the end of it. At the right side of the check there is a box with a dollar sign next to it ($). You write the amount of the check numerically. For example: $134.00. If you need to write a memo there is a line for this in the bottom left hand corner. Finally, you sign the check in the bottom right hand corner. Then you tear out the check.

Ordering Your Checks – Do not waste money here. You do not need to get checks that have your favorite cartoon character, if you have to pay more. They are not very professional anyway. Most of the time check duplicates are a good idea.

ATM Fines – You need to plan your day so that you know ahead of time how much money you need. Plan so that you do not have to pay ATM fines if you can. Paying a ATM fine should be a rare thing that you almost never do.

Overdraft Fines – So you ran out of money. The bank has decided to fine you. Maybe you forgot to record a purchase. Pay it and get on with your life. Use you bank card as a debit to make it harder to overdraft.

Free May Be Costing You- Sometimes banks that offer many services for free, also, make you pay higher fines and fees on other services. All banks are not equal. Free may be the most expensive price.

Paying Your Bills- Put your bill account number in the memo section of your check. This helps the billing department where you send your payment to not get you confused with someone else.

Don't Confuse Your Friendly IRS Agent -Keep all your business and personal accounts separate.

Give Yourself A Salary - Don't work for yourself for free. You wouldn't work for anyone else for free. If your business is new it may not be able to pay you right away. Keep track of your hours. You can recompense yourself later. Even if you plan on making your business an asset, do this.

Chapter

29

Just Start

Money Story-Simple Simon has a friend named Winnie Wisdom. She is a friend to Simple Simon. He, however, ignores her. Simple Simon's house needs painting. The job seems to big for Simple Simon so he leaves it undone. Winnie Wisdom gets her house painted every year all by herself. She tells Simon the "secret"- Just start! True to form Simon ignores Winnie because it is - "too much work".

Do Not Wait For Lightning To Strike - If you are waiting for your circumstances to get better you may be wasting valuable time. Most circumstances will not get better unless you do something to change them. Just start with what you have. If you don't known what you are doing it is probably still better than doing nothing. Time is much more important than money. No matter what other people think.

You Don't Have to Know Everything- Surround yourself with people who are experts in their field or who at least know what they are doing.
Money Verses -
"He that observeth the wind shall not sow; and he that regardeth the clouds shall not reap." Ecclesiastes11:4

"The slothful man saith, There is a lion without, I shall be slain in the streets." Proverbs 22:13

Enthusiasm May Be The Key - Do not be overwhelmed by the amount of work to be done. So you did not realize how much work there is to this. Just start somewhere. Make yourself accountable to someone. Put together a step-by-step plan to reach your goal if you think that will help.

You Can't See the Forest Because of the Trees

Sometimes opportunity is hard to see in the business world simply because there are so many successful businesses and business people. There seems to be no room to grow a new business, but do not be discouraged. Even a mighty oak started out as an acorn.

Organize Your Life – Make a list of your priorities. Your **REAL** priorities. Make sure you balance your life correctly. You only get to live it once.

Good New Ideas are Hard to Come By

Investors love new ideas. If you have an idea that is truly original you may be able to pitch it to a group of investors and start a company. You could also sell your idea if you do not want the headache of starting your own business. To do that though you will probably have to patent (or show legal ownership of) the idea. This is a good way to start out in business. Even if you do not have money you can still have an idea. The engine, the light bulb, and many other things were once only ideas.

The Goal: From Survivor to Thriver- Once your company is set up with your hand picked, well trained, manager in place, you sit back and collect your profits.

- I hope that this small book will be helpful to you. Thank you for reading it. May the Lord bless you in your financial life.

Chapter

30

Who Really Is Rich?

Money Story
If two men were shipwrecked on an island and one man had ten-thousand dollars and the other had a cheeseburger which one would be considered truly rich?

Lesson Learned
Some things in life are worth much more than money, yet, those things can often be threatened by finances. Do not let **success or failure** change those things for worse. Decide that now.

Money Verses – "There is that maketh himself rich, yet hath nothing: there is that maketh himself poor, yet hath great riches."
Proverbs 13: 7

"For what is a man profited, if he shall gain the whole world and lose his own soul? or what shall a man give in exchange for his soul."
Matthew 16:26

Wisdom- This is the most important thing to learn in your life. It is more important than how much money you have in the bank or how much you're worth. There are many verses in the Bible that teach wisdom. Get this above all else.

Money Verse- "Happy is the man that findeth wisdom, and the man that getteth understanding. For the merchandise of it is better than the merchandise of silver, and the gain thereof than fine gold. She is more precious than rubies: and all the things thou canst desire are not to be compared unto her." Proverbs 3:13-15

Need a Mentor?

It is much easier to learn a business with a mentor then by trying to learn through trial and error. I do not recommend paying for a mentor. They might just be trying to get your money. If you do have a dream but no mentor you may just want to wait on that dream and start a new dream were you do have the type of mentor(for your new endeavor) already available to you. Remember, you need only to learn how to run a business once. Then, you will be trained to be a success for most other businesses. You can always return to your original dream.

Money Verse- "He that walketh with wise men shall be wise: but a companion of fools shall be destroyed." Proverbs 13:20

Make Friends with Your Banker- This may sound silly but it is often overlooked. Your banker has valuable knowledge that he is often willing to share. You may want to get close to this person. He can be your most valuable counselor. He may not always be right. Yet, his business is money. He probably understands his business. More often than not my banker is right.

Appendix

Questions to ask when making a business plan:

What do you sell?

What time are you opened?

What time is peak time?

How many hours do you need to be staffed?

How many employees do you need to hire?

Can you trust your employees?

Do you need a security camera?

How much do your employee's make?

How much rent can you afford?

How much foot traffic do you have?

How much advertising do you need?

How much does your supplier charge per unit?

What is your mark up?

Are you conveniently located?

Would it be better to own or rent?

How much should you charge for your trouble?

How much tax do you pay?

How much profit do you make?

How much profit do you need to cover your expenses?

Does your place need repair?

Can you add new product to your business?

Is there anything unique about your business?

Can someone undersell you?

Can you cut costs without undermining the integrity of your business?

What is your big seller?

How much insurance do you need?

Do you have debt?

Do you need utilities?

Do you need equipment?

How much do you have in expenses?

How much do you have to sell to make a profit?

Can you make a profit?

Is your profit in percentages?

Do you take returns?

These are by no means all the things you need to ask, but, they are intended to get you started.

Do you know for sure if you died today that you would go to heaven?

Do not let riches come between you and God! No one is so successful that they don't need God. Rejecting God is the single biggest mistake that the rich make.

The Bible says:

He also that received seed among the thorns is he that heareth the word; and the care of this world, and the <u>deceitfulness of riches</u>, choke the word, and he becometh unfruitful. Matthew 13:22*(note: my underline)*

<u>Do you agree with God?</u>

Many, many rich people think they do not need God because they have riches. They are deceived by riches.

This type of rich person will not get saved because he is rich or because he wants riches.

The Bible says:

And again I say unto you, It is easier for a camel to go through the eye of a needle, then for a rich man to enter into the kingdom of God Matthew 19:24

<u>Do you agree with God?</u>

Heaven is a perfect place. Nothing sinful can enter heaven. Have you ever sinned?

A sin is breaking one of God's laws. For example: the Ten Commandments.

The Bible says:

"For all have sinned, and come short of the glory of God;" Romans 3:23

<u>Do you agree with God?</u>

The Bible says:

"For the wages of sin is death;" Romans 6:23a

That means someday you will die. That is the price of sin.

Do you agree with God?

Have you ever lied and said something that you know was not true?

The Bible says:

"Yea, let God be true, but every man a liar;" Romans 3:4

Do you agree with God?

The Bible says

"and all liars, shall have their part in the lake which burneth with fire and brimstone: which is the second death." Rev 21:8

Clearly, if that were the end of the story, we would be in trouble.

Do you agree with God?

"But God commendeth his love toward us, in that, while we were yet sinners, Christ died for us." Romans 5:8

Jesus came to earth in the form of a little baby. His mother was a Virgin named Mary. God was His Father. He lived a perfect life. He died on a cross. Yet, three days later He came back to life from the dead. Later, he left earth to join God in heaven. He promised to return to gather his believers.

God showed his love in a strong way. While he knew we were all bad people, He sent His Son Jesus to pay our death and hell on the cross. Now our sins have been paid for. In the sight of God we as Christians are now perfect.

Are you a Christian?

You can be a Christian!

Heaven is a free gift.

The Bible says:

"But not as the offence, so also is the free gift." Romans 5:15

"but the gift of God is eternal life Christ our Lord." Romans 6:23b

Do you agree with God?

All that you have to do is accept the free gift by placing all of your faith in Christ.

How do you do that?

All the faith that you need is simply the faith that it takes to pray – you only need to ask Christ once for that free gift of heaven.

The Bible says:

"For whosoever shall call upon the name of the Lord shall be saved." Romans 10:13

This is not like calling a friend to come here. It is more like you're at the top of your building and it is on fire. The firemen do not see you and you're calling the fire men to rescue you. That is the type of calling.

Do you agree with God?

By faith right now ask Jesus for his gift of heaven.

Here is a sample prayer - personalize it and make it yours

Jesus will you please right now cleanse me from my sin. Will you take me to heaven when my time comes and I die? Thank you for preparing a place for me, amen.

Once you have prayed this prayer in faith

"Jesus saith unto him, I am the way," John 14:6

It is his way or no way at all.

If there was any other way to get to heaven Christ's death on the cross would be worthless.

He said, "and him that cometh to me I will in no wise cast out." John 6:37b

He also said, "I will never leave thee, nor forsake thee." Hebrews 13:5 *Jesus will be with you forever and never leave you. That means you can no longer go to hell. Faith is the knowledge that the creator of the universe loves me more than life itself and will take care of me in this life and ultimately in the next.*

The next step in your new life in Christ is baptism. It does not make you a Christian, but, it represents to the world that you are now a Christian. If you were baptized as a child you should be rebaptized once you have become a believer. When you are baptized you need to join a Bible believing church and attend faithfully. I recommend most Independent Fundamental Baptist Churches though not all of them. If you need to find one, look in the phone book or online.

101 Ways to Save Money

Proverbs 18:9; Proverbs 21:20

1. Use generic products
2. Shop stores that match prices of competitor stores.
3. Save coupons - don't go shopping when you're hungry!
4. Tailor your weekly meals according to what's on sale.
5. Use cheapest grade gasoline your car recommends.
6. Do your own oil changes and car washes. Change your own headlights and washer blades.
7. Just say "no" to add-on car repairs.
8. Do you need full auto coverage?
9. Raise deductible on homeowner's insurance - $1,000
10. Raise deductible on health insurance - $1,200?
11. Only buy term life insurance.
12. Mail in those rebates (40% don't)
13. Winterize your home - windows - clear plastic.
14. Add attic insulation - buy it on sale before winter
15. Plug in all exterior outlets
16. Keep thermostat at 66-68 degrees in winter.
17. Keep air conditioning at 75 degrees in summer.
18. Fix leaky faucets/ toilets.
19. Use ceiling fans on low speed (force heat down and cool up)
20. Cut your own grass (cheap $100.00 mower is sufficient)
21. Shovel own snow (unless health problems)
22. Hire own maintenance people for home repairs (recommended by a friend)
23. Keep all filters clean - furnace - washable type
      Air conditioner - keep dirt out (take back off & clean)
      Car - air filter
      Dryer - vacuum back
      Vacuum - bag change
24. Never trade your car in - sell it yourself! Keep it until it's done. (Last for - 200k miles)
25. Buy 5 year old used cars at 20% of new MRSP
  Ex. 60k miles - Ford Chevy Dodge @ $3,500-6,000 range
   Worst resale value car - KIA
26. Shop thrift stores carefully
27. Trade clothes with a friend. Ex. Ties
28. Wear clothes until dirty.
29. Wear hair until dirty - dandruff caused by washing out oil
30. Use roll on stick deodorants.
31. Buy electric razor - $30.00 cordless - save on razors/cream
32. Buy hair clippers - mothers - cut boys' hair!
33. Stop carrying extra cash!
34. Never pay ATM fees – Use card for emergencies - 1st time overdraft - get rid of card
35. Use totally free checking accounts
36. Credit cards - fear them!
  Use 0% financing - but don't be late!
  Keep balances under 50% of credit limits
  Never use for cash advances
37. Stop eating out - if you do - discover the 99 cents menu and a cup of water
38. Stop eating sugar - ice cream, cakes, pies, candy bars; expensive and unhealthy
39. Stop drinking pop - drink more water.

40 Stop playing lottery - designed to be played by those who don't know math (it feeds greed)

41. Stop buying a newspaper - $325.00/year for what, to get depressed?

42. Stop buying snacks - gas stations make biggest profits?

43. Stop smoking - thousands of dollars/year to die a torturous death?!

44. Stop running to the doctor.

45. Don't get divorced.

46. Turn your water heater to a lower setting - take shorter showers.

47. Use florescent bulbs 13 w - 75 w light $2.50 saves you $39.00 each bulb.

48. Cancel cable television or satellite dish -free television , library videos instead.

49. Use 1,000 sheet toilet paper - dishrags instead of paper towels

50. Use Dryel sheets or Dry Cleaner's Secret - do own dry cleaning!

51. Recycle everything possible. Folks who lived through depression have a hard time throwing stuff away.

   Magazines and books are given away at library

   Video tapes for $1.00

   Make someone else's trash your treasure

   Aluminum cans - .43 cents a lb. = $6 - $7 a load

52. Consult Consumer Reports before buying major purchases.

   Cars, appliances, etc. - Buying guide at library

53. Shop yard sales, garage sales, classified ads

   Don't be afraid to haggle! Most expect you to!

54. Always watch store clerks and cashiers carefully - double check receipts!

55. Buy checks through the mail

   Bank ordered checks cost you more than double! (May need extra deposit slips)

56. Do not make late fees - pay them if you do.

   Use grace period if needed.

   If it's a choice between credit card and mortgage payment both due on the first, make the mortgage payment a little late. Dirty little secret - If you're late on other loans, the bank can raise your credit card rates! Fear them!

57. Use calling cards or tracfones instead of cell phones

   Cell phone contracts are expensive!

58. Avoid tickets/ accidents

   Drive speed limit

   If you do a lot of highway driving, get a radar detector where legal. The problem isn't just the ticket, the insurance rate goes up for 3 years.

59. Car pool - combine errands into 1 trip and walk if under a mile (8 blocks)

60. Check tire pressure frequently

   (More during winter months)

   Save gas and save wear on tires

   Have tires rotated every 6,000 miles (if free)

61. Consider home schooling - instead of Christian school tuition!

62. Consider doing your own taxes. Save with turbo tax or software program. Go long form - if you own a home, if you're tithing (turn in receipts of donations)

63. Consider setting up a bi-weekly mortgage payment. Direct withdrawal - save thousands.

64. Pay a little extra on your current mortgage payment each month.

   Ex. $550 instead of $500 a month. The extra $50 cuts off nearly 10 years in payments and $48,000 in interest

65. File for all deductions possible on your property taxes.

   Ex. Senior citizen discount

   Primary residence

   Mortgage deduction

66. Buy a home according to your needs - not wants!

   Most people don't need a 3,000+ square foot house with 3+ bathrooms.

   Nothing wrong with finishing your life in a starter home.

Keep mortgage payment at 25% or less of your income

Buy a fixer upper and put in sweat equity (Double their value overnight)

67. Check into combining auto and homeowners' insurance with the same company.

   Many give additional discounts if they carry both.

   Don't hesitate to shop around for best rates.

68. Turn off the AC and turn the heat way down when away for more than a day.

   Two possible suggestion when away – 80 degrees for AC, 50 degrees for heat.

69. Check your house for drafts.

   Weatherstrip leaky doors/windows

   Check each vent for possible holes in duct work under the house, when the furnace isn't running.

   Draft dodgers for door bottoms

70. When replacing water fixtures, switch to water-saving types.

   Low water usage shower heads.

   Low flush toilets

   Good garden hoses- nozzles that don't drip

71. Whenever replacing appliances - try to get energy saving ones.

   Ex. Certain washing machines take less water and energy to run.

72. Use alternative heat whenever possible

   Especially if you live in the country!

   A wood stove can save thousands

   Pellet stoves - burn paper /wood/corn pellets

      $350 vs. $2000

   Some wood stoves give you hot water year round.

   Check with your insurance company before purchasing

73. Buy in bulk products that you like (never buy 1 of anything)

   Cans of food on sale - buy 6 to 24 if you have space and money (be sure to rotate stock)

   (Goal price – 33cents a can)

   Shop Sam's Club - Costco - possible food co-op

74. Cut down to two meals a day(for you not your kids)

   You'll save money - lose weight

   Try fasting 1 day a week(also for you not your kids)

   Make one meal a 1 food meal a day

   Eat little or no meat for one meal

75. Buy bottled water in the gallon size.

   Ex. Ice Mount in clear 1 gallon - $2.45 cold

   Next time fill it half up - freeze it - then fill all the way up before taking with you. (Keep repeating).

76. Go fish! (Or hunting)

   Go collect blackberries and raspberries, etc. (Also walnuts, cherries, asparagus, mushrooms - if knowledgeable) Apples will often just rot on ground.

77. Learn to love leftovers

   Surveys show Americans throw out twice as much food as 20 years ago

   Idea - Save small amounts of leftover veggies. Combine with other leftovers in containers in the freezer. Use at one time in soups, pot pies, etc.

   Idea - put a slice of cheese on leftover mashed potatoes, add 1 tablespoon of butter and 1/4 teaspoon garlic powder; reheat and serve.

78. Keep the freezer full!

   It actually costs less to operate than a half empty one.

   It also stays colder longer if power goes out.

79. Cut out the desserts

   Desserts are expensive and unhealthy

   Bag your own lunch for work

   Stop buying that Starbuck's and Krispy Kreme!

80. Order take out at buffets instead of dining in.
    Ex. Ryan's - get a Styrofoam tray & pay for food by the pound.
    It is cheaper , you'll eat less and save the tip.
81. Plant a garden
    Freeze or give away extra
82. Learn to sew
83. Buy panty hose 1 size larger than you need
    They'll last longer
    Buy the three pack (if cheaper)
84. Buy good quality shoes on sale
    Often fit your feet better
    Later can possibly be resoled.
85. Substitute for household products when money is tight.
    Dishwashing liquid for shampoo
    Baking soda for toothpaste
    Vinegar and water for window cleaner
    Newspapers for paper towels for windows
    Vaseline for gel or mousse to stop frizzies
    (Barely touch finger in jar - rub hands - work into your hair)
86. Discover the numerous uses of hydrogen peroxide.
    Use carefully as a mouthwash and teeth brightener
    Disinfectant to clean counters, cutting boards, door knobs, etc.
    Use 50/50 with water to spray on feet to kill nail fungus and athlete's feet
    A cup added to laundry instead of bleach whitens clothes
    Soak toothbrushes in it to sanitize
    Soak cuts and infections 5-10 minutes daily
    A more natural hair highlighter.
    Add small amount to pet's water to kill germs and add oxygen
    Kills yeast infections
87. Use silk flowers instead of fresh
    For table settings, grave sites, home decorations (can be rotated according to season)
    (Not recommended for wife's birthday or anniversary!)
88. Make your own Christmas and birthday gifts.
    More meaningful to some folks.
    Use gift bags given to you instead of wrapping paper
89. Buy or pick up a cheap, artificial Christmas tree.
    Look for free ones on curb after Christmas
90. Buy merchandise off season
    Christmas decorations - 75% off
    Winter clothes on sale before spring
    Vacations can be half price at many places off season
91. Wait (a year or so) for the newest high tech gadgets to drop in price
    Plasma TV, DVD, MP3, Bluetooth, Xbox
92. Develop simple tastes in entertainment
    Play at the park
    Walk by lake front/forest preserve
    DVD purchased for $1
    Trip to library
93. Buy slightly damaged or demo products at retail stores
    Products without a box - don't hesitate to ask for a discount
    Groceries just before expiration date
    New demo cars
94. Check out slightly bruised automobiles
    Repo's; stolen vehicles; wrecked or water damaged (be sure water level wasn't high)

Www.autonetworkinc.com
95. Barter your time/services
    Ex. You cut grass - they'll babysit.
    You run to store or errand - they shovel your snow
    You're a plumber - neighbor is a mechanic
96. Consider renting out a room, basement, garage, shed or side/backyard space.
    No teens brought into home if you have teens. No young adults if you're a young couple.
97. Carefully consider renting your RV, vacation cabin or your home during winter.
    You may even be able to house sit for someone for 6 months while they're down south.
98. Always file receipts for new purchases
    You'll need them for warranties, to exchange item if it breaks, and possibly for taxes.
99. Donate to charity
    Old cars, furniture, clothes, musical instruments, etc.
    Goodwill/Amvets gives tax write off receipts. (kars4kids.com)
100. Give to others regularly
    You receive joy and helps control own covetousness.
101. TITHE!
    Mal. 3:10,11 - God blesses and 90% will stretch further

www.ingramcontent.com/pod-product-compliance
Lightning Source LLC
Chambersburg PA
CBHW071248170526
45165CB00003B/1277